Running for Judge

Running for Judge

Campaigning on the Trail of Despair, Deliverance and Overwhelming Success

TIM FALL

Foreword by Renee Branson

RESOURCE *Publications* • Eugene, Oregon

RUNNING FOR JUDGE
Campaigning on the Trail of Despair,
Deliverance and Overwhelming Success

Resource Publications
An Imprint of Wipf and Stock Publishers
199 W. 8th Ave., Suite 3
Eugene, OR 97401

www.wipfandstock.com

PAPERBACK ISBN: 978-1-7252-6087-0
HARDCOVER ISBN: 978-1-7252-6086-3
EBOOK ISBN: 978-1-7252-6088-7

Manufactured in the U.S.A.   02/03/20

To Liz, who sticks by me.
She's Proverbs 18:24, 2 Corinthians 1:3–4,
and 1 Corinthians 13:8 all wrapped up in one.

Contents

Foreword | ix
by Renee Branson

Preface | xiii

Chapter 1 | 1
The Phone Call

Chapter 2 | 6
A Young Judge with Imposter Syndrome:
The First Thirteen Years

Chapter 3 | 17
Family Matters

Chapter 4 | 22
An Assault on Lungs and Brain

Chapter 5 | 30
Law School, Lawyering, and
the Fellowship of Judging

Chapter 6 | 45
Church

Chapter 7 | 52
Campaign

Chapter 8 | 72
Self Care

Chapter 9 | 78
The Fall Guy

Chapter 10 | 84
Home Stretch

Chapter 11 | 91
Election Day

Chapter 12 | 103
Aftermath and Lessons Learned

Epilogue | 119
A Parable and an Encouragement

Postscript | 122

Foreword

I MET TIM FALL in the most modern of ways: through Twitter. He is a judge and I am a mental health professional who works within the legal industry. I didn't immediately make that connection, however. It was Tim's expression of his faith and his efforts to invite more diverse voices into conversation that resonated with me. He doesn't shy away from hard questions and tough conversations, traits I recognize in the most resilient people. In my work, I define resilience as the ability to bounce forward from crisis, challenge, and change. It allows us to perform well while in the midst of crisis, while we learn continuously through the process. Resilient is also the perfect word to describe Judge Tim Fall's story. A deeply personal story, it is also a story that I hear recounted in different ways, sometimes with more difficult endings, many times over from lawyers and other legal professionals.

I've been working in the field of resilience for over twenty years. First as a classroom educator, then as a therapist, and now working exclusively within the legal profession, I help people cultivate resilient practices and cultures. During the early part of my career, I worked with survivors of trauma: child abuse, sexual assault, war, and accidents. I became fascinated by what allowed some survivors to bounce forward from their trauma more easily than others in similar situations (although it is never truly "easy".)

What made some not only survive, but thrive beyond their experience? In other words, what makes people resilient? What I have discovered is that while we each may have a certain, predetermined level of resilience—much like the color of our eyes or how tall we are—there are factors fully within our control that will allow us to stretch and grow our resilience. Likewise, there are factors that create barriers to our resilience. One such barrier is the shame derived from stigma. Researcher Brene Brown defines shame as the "intensely painful feeling of believing we are flawed and therefore unworthy of love, belonging, and connection." The stigma in our culture around mental health, especially within the legal profession, creates shame and, thus, fear in seeking help.

Pushing the realities of mental health and substance abuse into the dark corners make it less likely for lawyers to practice resilience behaviors. Indeed, the opposite. Lawyers are nearly four times more likely to suffer from depression, anxiety, and substance abuse than other professions. There are many factors that contribute to this epidemic. The extremely long work hours, pressures of the billable hour, the competitive, adversarial, and isolating nature of the profession, a culture of drinking, and the unique "lawyer mind set" of skepticism, introversion, and perfectionism all add to a recipe that can both exacerbate existing mental health challenges and create environments for new illnesses to emerge. It was my own introduction to the quiet suffering in the profession that lead me to work exclusively within the legal profession. Four years ago, I met with a managing partner at a prestigious law firm in Washington D.C. I was there not as a therapist; I was on a fundraising visit for a nonprofit. As I settled into the large boardroom overlooking the Capital, this powerful partner looked across the table, smiled, and said, "I read that you are a therapist or something like that." He had clearly done his due diligence on finding out who was going to be asking him for a donation that day, I thought. His smile faded and he continued, "I need you to know that this profession is killing us." I sat back in my chair. "This profession is killing us." The flash of desperation in his eyes that told me he wasn't making a flippant remark about a singularly stressful day. "This profession is killing us." Honestly, I don't remember if I got around to asking him for a donation. I hope that something about our conversation changed the trajectory of his experience. I know without a doubt that it changed mine. Until that point, most of my clients had been, in one way or another, from marginalized populations. I met with women in domestic violence shelters and held play therapy sessions with children who were in foster care. Most services I provided were free to the clients. What I discovered that day in that exquisite law firm office, was that not by nature of economic circumstance, race, or gender, but by professional stigma, this seemingly powerful person had been made to feel powerless to his circumstances. To this day, I am humbled and grateful that he found the courage to speak his truth on that particular day. I am likewise humbled and grateful that Tim Fall is sharing his story with us.

When we own our stories, not only are we empowered by them, those stories make space for others to show up in their authenticity as well. This is why Tim's memoir is so vital and will contribute to the changing dynamics in the legal profession. His work is part of a larger movement to make the practice of law and the judicial system one that embraces well-being so that professionals thrive in their practice. Tim brings his personal account of anxiety out of the dark corners in a way that is moving, hopeful, and yes, resilient. He illustrates how he not only survives with anxiety, but thrives with it, using the lessons it has taught him to expand his compassion, empathy, and ability to serve justice. He wants to light a path for others so that they might cultivate their own resilience. It is my belief that by his testimony, in a faith-base and justice-based sense, others will be encouraged and uplifted to own their own stories and embrace a practice of well-being as well.

Renee Branson, MA, CReC
RB Consulting, LLC

Preface

You don't often hear or read of elected officials who are battling mental illness. When Thomas Eagleton's treatment for depression became public knowledge, it put an end to his role as George McGovern's running mate in 1972. Other politicians took note that disclosing mental illness can end your career. Speaking of it after retirement might be acceptable, but no one running for office wants to try to convince voters to cast ballots for someone who is mentally ill.

Stigma is a problem, but I am here to tell you that mental illness does not disqualify. A quarter of our population has anxiety, depression, or both, but they are not thereby unable to be productive and effective on the job, in their families, or around their communities.

I wrote this book—at least in part—to prove this true. This is a mental health memoir even more than a memoir of a judicial election. My 2008 reelection is merely the framework upon which to place the truths I've learned about mental illness and about myself.

Judges, as much as anyone else, carry huge responsibilities. I am living proof that anxiety and depression do not disqualify one from carrying out those responsibilities. My experience also proves that these are not to be carried alone. Faith, family, friends and good medical care are part of the process for addressing mental illness.

If you battle mental illness or know someone who does (and you do, statistics show), others may try to convince you that mental illnesses like depression and anxiety are all in your head. I suggest you tell them this: "Of course mental illness is all in your head. And a heart attack is all in your chest. Go see a doctor either way."

That's what I tell people, and after you read this book you might feel better able to tell them that yourself.

Chapter 1

The Phone Call

I STEPPED OFF THE bench for the lunch recess and saw the message light on my phone in chambers. Judges don't get a lot of voicemail. Phone calls usually reach our clerk's desk and stop there. This one didn't.

It was a reporter from the largest of our small county's local papers, a good writer whose work I respect. She knew a lot about the courts and learned even more after she married Mike, one of the more experienced attorneys in the Public Defender's office. Lauren only called about administrative matters. She knows judges can't talk about their cases. I didn't know of anything newsworthy going on with court administration so when the message started and I heard who it was I was a bit stumped.

"Hi, Judge. It's Lauren at the Enterprise. I'm on deadline and wondering if you can call me back by 3:00."

Still stumped.

"I'm hoping you can give me a response to Jim Walker's announcement that he's planning to run against you this year." Then she left her number.

⁓

I didn't call back right away. I couldn't. I found my heart was racing, my breath was shallow, my hands shook, and somehow I was yawning. Uncontrollable yawning. Big gaping yawns that had no connection to my state of wakefulness, because after that telephone call I was wide awake.

I did what judges do when faced with something big. I stepped back to think it over. I left chambers and walked out into the marble-walled hallways of the 90-year-old neo-classical courthouse, out the heavy brass and glass doors, down the broad granite courthouse steps, onto the pathway through the lawn under the spreading pine trees. My back to the courthouse, I kept walking away. All the way to the post office across the street. I had some letters to mail.

Performing mundane tasks is one of my go-to coping mechanisms. If I can't get started on a big project I'll take on something small to prime the pump. This works well until I let the small items displace the big one. In this case I figured I'd walk across the street, mail the letters, and—with my head cleared—prepare my thoughts for that return phone call. And who knew? Maybe there'd been some mistake. The rumors had been that Walker, a prosecutor a year or two older than I am, was thinking of challenging one of the newer judges.

It wasn't a mistake, as I found out when I returned to the base of the courthouse steps. There was Jim Walker, coming up the side path from the District Attorney's office. I considered bolting up the steps at the sight of him but stopped myself and turned his way. Our eyes met over the distance. Then he stopped and turned away from me as if returning to his office.

"Mr. Walker," I called out to his retreating back, "do you have a moment?"

"Sure," he said, and turned my way with half a smile on his face.

"I heard you're planning on running for judge. Who'd you decide to run against?"

The half smile broadened slightly. "You, I guess."

~

On the way back to chambers I thought "What does he mean 'I guess'? I guess?!"

My head was plenty clear to talk to Lauren now. I checked the clock over my clerk's desk in chambers and saw there was some time left before the afternoon session would start.

"Hi, Lauren. It's Judge Fall. Is this a good time?" Clear voice, even tone, measured pace. Good, I thought, no yawning. I'm doing OK.

"I was wondering about your response to Jim Walker's announcement," she said.

"Your phone call was the first I heard about it. When did this happen?"

Lauren filled me in. Walker had been building up to this for a while, got the support of the head of a political group in Woodland, our county seat, and made his announcement at one of their meetings.

"Judgeships aren't partisan in California," I said. "He announced this at a political party meeting?"

"He did. He sent out a press release, too," she said. "So, I called you to hear what you have to say for the article."

"Are you ready?"

She was.

"I've been a judge since 1995," I said, launching into an impromptu oral resume. "In thirteen years I've handled every kind of case there is, from small claims to first degree murder. I've been the Presiding Judge of the courthouse and Assistant Presiding Judge before that, been appointed by the Chief Justice of the California Supreme Court to serve on statewide judicial committees, and I teach judicial ethics to judges from the Oregon state line to the Mexican border."

I was on a roll, so I took a deep breath and continued, "I've served this court and county well, and I think that's why no one has thought to challenge me in thirteen years. If he wants to run against me, I'm ready." I wasn't sure I was ready. "The democratic process is a good one."

There was silence on my end while I heard computer keys clacking over the phone.

"Do you need anything else?" I asked when the clacking stopped.

"That's plenty."

"Can I go off the record for a moment?"

"Of course." Lauren was always good about allowing off the record conversations. If she needed to, she'd ask to go back on the record. "What's up?"

"I'm going to bury him."

"You think so?"

"My plan is to get support from everyone I can think of. Campaign from one side of the county to the other, and win with at least 60% of the vote."

"60%? You think that high?"

"I do. At least." I took a breath. "You have a 3:00 deadline? So I need to look for this in tomorrow's paper."

"That's my editor's plan."

"Call me if you need anything else. And say hi to Mike for me." I hung up.

Then the yawning returned.

〜

Tracee has been (and continues to be) the only clerk assigned to my chambers in all my years as a judge. We work well together and at over a dozen years on the bench by then I'd come to rely on her skills in managing court files, attorney phone calls, and making sure the daily schedule ran on time. Her desk sits only a few feet from mine, a visual and physical assurance that when it comes to courtroom and chambers matters everything will be as ready as possible for the hearings and cases set before me.

It's a good thing she's good at her job, because after that phone call it was all I could do to just sit at my desk trying to stifle the resuming yawns, my mind racing with thoughts about how on earth I was going to carry off the campaign I'd just described to Lauren, and when I'd get the time to call Liz, my wife, and tell her. So, with me sitting rooted at my desk, racing thoughts in my head and my mouth gaping with incessant yawning, Tracee hit the buzzer from the courtroom reminding me the afternoon calendar was ready to be called.

I stood, reached for my robe, pulled it on and zipped it closed all the way to my throat as I walked to the door leading to the courtroom, opening it up directly behind my seat at the bench. I lowered myself safely into the large wing-backed chair, stopped yawning, and was able to handle the cases set for hearing that afternoon.

The last case finally concluded, I returned to chambers and hung up the robe. As I did, the yawning returned. The large, incessant gaping yawns. Where were these coming from? A phrase I once heard entered my mind.

Stress yawn.

Is that a thing?

I looked it up. It's a thing.

Stress causes the body to tense, breathing to become shallow, and the heart to beat faster. For some reason, yawning is one of the body's responses to these physical events. I later learned that dogs sometimes yawn for the same reason. They get stressed by odd circumstances—a stranger talking to a family member, a big dog walking by—and will yawn. I like dogs. If they stress yawn, it can't be all bad.

But why was I so stressed? I truly believed what I told Lauren. I was going to win and win big. My brain knew this. Why didn't my body go along?

Chapter 2

A Young Judge
with Imposter Syndrome

The First Thirteen Years

I PUT IN MY application for a judgeship only six years out from law school graduation in 1987. Back then, California still had Municipal Courts and anyone who had been a member of the State Bar for at least five years was eligible either for a Governor's appointment to an open seat or for election to the bench. Superior Court judges needed ten years. Judges serve in a particular county but are state officers rather than local officials.

A seat opened in my county when a Municipal Court judge was elevated to the Superior Court, and I hoped to get the appointment to take her place. The application form alone is daunting: ten pages, single-spaced, asking for personal information dating back years, professional and social information, plus a list of references. Once that's submitted, the next step is to obtain letters of recommendation. This is where putting in hard work as a lawyer pays off because other attorneys, local officials, and community leaders tend to take judgeships seriously. They won't put their name on a recommendation if they don't think you're right for the job. But if they do think you're right for it they'll not only write a letter to the

Governor but also connect you with others whose opinions the Governor listens to.

If the Governor's office thinks you're worth a closer look, they send your name to the State Bar's Judicial Nominee Evaluation (JNE, pronounced Jenny) Commission. About six months after I applied, the Governor sent a list of names of people applying for that one judgeship to the JNE Commission for evaluation.

My name wasn't on the list.

I called the administrative assistant in the Governor's appointments office. An older woman with the kindest voice, she'd been my contact, guiding me in making sure I had everything in order, always ready for my questions about the application process, so I called her and asked my latest question.

"Mrs. Miller, it's Tim Fall. Am I dead in the water?"

"Oh my. No, Tim, I wouldn't say you're dead in the water," she said gently. "No decisions have been made."

"What do I do now, Mrs. Miller? Just wait?"

"I think that's best. Nothing's decided until someone's appointed."

I waited. Month after month, I waited. It turned out no appointment came from that initial list of six applicants. The Governor's office never explains why someone doesn't get the appointment but some people suspected the reason all six people on this list were passed over had to do with the fact the Appointments Secretary (the head of the Governor's appointments office) was running for a seat in the state Assembly and concentrated on getting himself elected rather than filling open judge seats. He won and left the Governor's office for the legislative branch.

Eventually a new Appointments Secretary came in. It turned out he was on the University of California's Board of Regents and I knew three other members of the board: one of my old law professors, the managing partner of a law firm in Sacramento I'd had some cases with, and an expert witness I worked with on a lawsuit. Before these three became Regents, I had known none. In the time since they all left the Board of Regents, I've known none. But at the moment the new Appointments Secretary arrived in the Governor's office, I knew three Regents.

I called all of them and asked if they'd put in a good word for me with their fellow Regent, the new Appointments Secretary. They all said they would see him at the next board meeting. One of them told me to send a letter to him at the Governor's office to introduce myself and express my continued interest in a judgeship.

Whenever you send a letter to the Governor's office about a judicial application you receive a form letter in reply.

"We have received your application. Thank you."

"We have received your updated contact information. Thank you."

"We have received your most recent letters of recommendation. Thank you."

Each letter has a stamped signature from whoever the Appointments Secretary is at the time.

I sent in the letter introducing myself. The form letter came back. "We have received your letter indicating continued interest in a judicial appointment. Thank you." The Appointment Secretary's signature was stamped at the bottom. It was the handwritten margin note that jumped out at me. "Tim, I heard from Ward, Bob and Dan at the last Regent meeting. Looking forward to meeting you, John."

A month later, over a year after first submitting my application, my name finally made it onto a list sent to the JNE Commission. The Commission in turn asked me for names, addresses and phone numbers of 75 lawyers and judges I wanted them to send evaluation forms to. They would send out on their own yet another 100 evaluation forms to others in the legal field as well. After the evaluations came back they scheduled an interview for me to sit down with two Commission members.

Before the interview, the Commission sent me a letter identifying areas of concern I should be prepared to talk about. The first concern? Someone told them I was typically unprepared for court appearances. That, I thought, was weird. And while that one was weird, the second concern was horrifying: I was accused of treating women poorly.

I stood up from my desk in my law office and walked into Carolee's office next door with the JNE letter. Carolee is one of the partners of this firm I'd worked at since graduating law school, and I needed her advice on responding to this accusation. After all, Carolee had been my mentor since the day I started. If anyone knew me as an attorney, she did.

"First," she said, "tell them the part about you being unprepared isn't true. Unless they give you specifics there's no more you can say."

"All right, but . . ."

"The part about women isn't true either. Tell them I said so. But you'll also need to talk about your experience as an attorney and how you interact with women. You don't want to let this get out of hand, especially since the letter says the two commissioners interviewing you are women."

I took Carolee's advice to heart, but I felt like I was driving without a map. All I knew was that people think I show up to court unprepared and don't treat women well. Great.

The interview day came.

Dressed in a suit and tie, shoes not too scuffed, hair not looking too off-kilter at the cowlicks (I have more than one at the back of my head and I think I sometimes look like I comb my hair with a towel), I entered a large conference room with long folding tables stretching its length and breadth. At the far end of the room, on the other side of the last table, sat my interlocutors.

Interlocutor is a fancy word even lawyers don't use often, but I hoped the session with these two women would be much more a conversation than an interrogation. And that's how it turned out. Most of it, anyway.

The young prosecutor from Santa Barbara took the lead while the older woman, a non-lawyer from Chico who was a JNE Commission veteran, smiled. It looked like they were working off a checklist. I suppose they need to evaluate every potential judge on the same basis. The older woman occasionally interjected a seemingly small question that actually pierced to the heart of whatever issue we'd been discussing.

Then they got to the big question.

"One criticism we received," the prosecutor said, "is about your treatment of women lawyers. Can you tell us about that?"

I measured my breath, tried not to sound defensive, and told them what Carolee told me to say. It didn't take long. It was essentially a sentence or two of me denying it by claiming I got along well with attorneys who also happen to be women. I finished with, "Unless there's something specific, I don't know what else to say."

"But," I paused as a new thought came to me, "there is one woman I had a tough time with. That was on a county bar committee, not in a courtroom."

"We can't get specific about who we spoke to," the prosecutor leaned across the table toward me, "but perhaps you could tell us more about that." She looked extremely interested in what I was about to say, like she'd been specifically waiting for this to come up.

The light bulb went on.

I'd served as an officer of the Yolo County Bar Association and had never clicked with one of the other officers. I told my interviewers that the cause had always been a mystery to me but I could definitely say that this was one instance where I'd admit to not getting along well with a woman attorney.

"I don't know what else to tell you about it."

"That's enough," the prosecutor said.

There was a long pause as I pretended to stare at my notes. The older commissioner was the one to lean across the table this time.

"We've heard a lot of nice things about you from people, too." She smiled and I thought she was about to pat my hand.

I looked again at the letter they'd sent. "So, this part about me not being prepared for court. That's just not . . ."

"I think we can skip that one." It was the prosecutor's turn to smile this time as she cut me off.

They explained the process that follows this interview. They'd report to the full Commission, the Commissioners would review all the evaluations and rate me on a scale—not qualified, qualified, well qualified, very well qualified—and send that rating to the Governor's office. No applicant receives notice of the JNE Commission's rating. The only inkling that you've been rated at least qualified to be a judge is if the Appointments Secretary's office calls you in for an interview.

Mrs. Miller called me in.

This interview was a cake walk in comparison. John, the Appointments Secretary, was an extremely nice man who had built a successful law practice over decades of serving the residents and legal community of San Diego. Taking this position in the Governor's office meant stepping back from his law practice but it was an opportunity to serve by providing a careful review of judicial applicants. I'd researched his background and saw the sacrifice he made to take the job at the request of his old friend, the Governor. When I entered his office and he invited me to sit I knew we had some common ground in wanting to serve.

The interview was about as I expected. We talked about my education, my law firm (he knew one of the founding partners), and my community work. At the end of our time he hit me with a question I should have seen coming.

"Why do you want to be a judge?"

"I've been in a lot of courtrooms up and down the state," I said and, before I could stop myself, I added, "and I think I can do a better job than some of the judges I've appeared in front of."

I shut my trap, appalled that he must think me—a 35-year-old with only seven and a half years' experience—the most arrogant applicant he'd ever interviewed. John's response surprised me.

"Ha! I think you're right!"

∽

A few weeks later I left work early to get home, change, and catch up with Liz and the kids to meet some friends for dinner at the local Wednesday night Farmer's Market. I was about to leave the house when the phone rang.

"Tim, this is John at the Governor's office." That would be John, the Appointments Secretary. "I tried to call you at work but they said you went home already."

Great, I thought. The Appointments Secretary now thinks I'm a shirker. There goes the judgeship. He was still talking.

"I wanted to let you know the Governor is issuing a press release tomorrow morning announcing your appointment."

I was wrong. Here *comes* the judgeship. A bit overcome, I managed a thank you. He laughed and there was a little more chit chat before we hung up.

A few deep breaths later I called Liz's cell phone.

"Hello?"

"May I speak to Judge Fall's wife?"

I think I could have heard the scream without benefit of the telephone.

～

Getting sworn in as a judge also means getting disbarred as an attorney. California law says that judges cannot hold licenses to practice law, so by virtue of taking the oath of judicial office I would automatically remove myself from the roll of licensed attorneys.

I called the State Bar and asked what would happen if I wanted to return to being an attorney after I stopped being a judge. My main concern was summed up in the question, "Would I have to take the bar exam all over again?" (That's a three-day, eighteen-hour, test in this state.)

She reassured me that they would let me right back in with no need to re-take the bar, since, as she put it, "We assume judges have stayed up on the law during their careers."

Whew.

It's not that I was planning on returning to law practice any time soon. I hoped to make judging my career until retirement. Still, it was nice to know I had the ability to fall back on being an attorney should this judging thing not work out. Yet even though I'd no longer be an attorney, I wouldn't stop being a lawyer. How can someone be a lawyer yet not an attorney, you might wonder?

Simple. An attorney is a person licensed by the government to practice law, to represent the interests of someone else in court or provide counsel to people needing legal advice.

A lawyer, on the other hand, is merely someone schooled in the law. That's me. That's also anyone else who graduated from law school, whether they ever went into the practice of law—or even passed the bar exam—or not. So, I'm a lawyer, but not an attorney.

Side note: since I'm not a licensed attorney, it's illegal for me to practice law, even for free . . . even for friends and family . . . even for people who just want to run something by me quickly on their legal issue. You don't know how many times I've had to explain this to people. *Sorry, I can't talk to you about your legal issues.* And then how many times I have to ask them to stop asking me questions about those legal issues. *No, I can't tell you how to get out of your traffic ticket/evict your tenant/plea bargain on your shoplifting charge/etc. Please stop asking me. Pretty please. Pretty please with sugar on top. Oh, for the love of Pete, LEAVE ME ALONE!"*

I've actually never said that last sentence out loud.

∾

Wrapping up work on files at my law firm and transferring them to other attorneys took a couple weeks. Finally, at 5:00 pm on July 31, 1995, I took the oath of judicial office.

I immediately felt like an imposter.

Every day I thought someone would tell me it was a mistake or, even worse, a joke. Out of all the applicants, what made me the right choice? Why pick me? It's a question that has dogged me from my childhood, like back in the fourth grade.

Fourth grade was an interesting time. And by interesting, I mean hard. Bullied often, beat up occasionally, and definitely not part of the in-crowd. Then again, I wasn't a complete pariah. I had some friends, most of whom were in the same boat. If one of the cool kids ever opened the inner circle wide enough to let me in, I always grabbed at the chance to step inside.

One day, we were supposed to be working at our desks on a set of questions about something we'd been studying. The teacher wasn't in the room at the time and a few of the kids started doing a different list of questions: something about your likes and dislikes.

One boy asked, "What about getting the questions done?"

A girl said, "Let's get Tim to do them?"

What I thought I'd heard was "Let's get Tim to answer these questions."

I set my worksheet down on my desk and walked over to the small group in the back of the room to take my turn at the questionnaire. Eventually the boy who wondered about getting the work done said, "Are you already done with the questions, Tim?"

I told them I hadn't even started. How could I, I thought, when they haven't asked me yet?

"Shouldn't you get on it? The teacher will be back soon."

It dawned on me. And so, rather than admit I thought they had invited me to join their inner circle—and still wanting to be part of their group even if not in the way I'd hoped—I said, "Yeah, it'll just take a minute."

I hurried through the worksheet and gave them the answers.

A different set of questions awaited me at the California Judicial College I attended after my appointment. For years, every judge attending the two-week college had been administered the Myers-Briggs personality test. I came out INTJ. That meant I was more introverted than extraverted, more inclined to intuition than sensing, more likely to rely on thinking than feeling, and prefer to exercise a judging function than a perceiving one. It was all so much babble to me, except for the way this plays out for judges. Our instructor explained that of the sixteen possible personality profile combinations of Myers-Briggs types, well over half of the judges in California fall into a single combination: INTJ, like I was then (I've more recently tested INFJ). Yet only two percent of the general population falls into this category. Perhaps that's why I felt an outcast when younger, and, when older, if not an outcast at least an oddball. Perhaps I'd found my people among the judiciary.

Rather than be an imposter, there was a chance I actually was cut out for this judging gig.

That doesn't mean judging is the easiest job, even for those of us supposedly wired for it. Judges hear awful things every day. Whether someone is the victim of a crime, seeking child custody or protesting having their child taken from them, suing for injuries in an accident or the one being sued, people who come to the courthouse are there because there is some crisis going on in their lives. I hear about death, theft, child abuse, rape, the ravages of drugs, or the toll mental illness takes on people and their loved ones, and I hear it in explicit detail.

Not everyone can do this job—and likewise there are a number of jobs I find unimaginable for me to do, too—but this job is the one that God has equipped and suited me for. In my early years on the bench, though, I was not yet convinced. Apparently, others wondered about me, too.

A few months after my appointment the filing period opened for the upcoming election. My upcoming election. I had been appointed to finish an open term and needed to successfully run for reelection for a new term in order to keep the job. The timeline was quick: sworn in on July 31, 1995, filing period opening that November, election in March 1996. This gave me no time to build a record as a judge, good or bad. I might be great or I might stink up the place but no one was going to know by Election Day.

A couple of months into the job I heard a rumor a local attorney thought of running against me. I went home that night in a near panic.

"Someone's talking about running for judge," I told Liz. "For my seat. Against me."

"OK." Liz can be quite understated.

"What if I lose? I like this job!"

"Tim, I don't think God put you in this position just to take you out of it right away," she said, "but what if he did? What are you going to do about it?"

She was right. She usually is.

It turned out the rumors came to nothing and I ran unopposed for a full six-year term, and the same again in 2002. For judges in California, running unopposed means not appearing on the ballot at all. No votes are cast. You're just declared the winner once the polls close on Election Day.

There are over 1500 trial court judges in California, and with staggered six-year terms that means that every election year finds over five hundred seats up for election. Typically, of those five hundred seats, fewer than two dozen judges in the state face a challenge in a given year, while there are plenty of races for seats left open when a judge has retired at the end of a term. That's where most attorneys will put their efforts if they'd rather run for judge and not go through the exhaustive and scrutinizing appointment process. Running for an open seat certainly has a more likely success rate, since defeating a judge at election only happens in one or two of the challenges mounted every election year.

For me and every one of my colleagues on our small court, no one filed to run against any of us in the six election seasons from 1996 to 2006. I had no reason to suspect 2008 would be any different.

Lauren's phone call told me otherwise.

Chapter 3

Family Matters

I WALKED IN THE door from our garage, the phone call from Lauren still fresh in my head. Liz was in the kitchen, Kyle was watching TV, Jenna was doing homework.

"I need all of you to stop for a minute. Let me know when you can."

Liz set down what she was working on, ran her hands under the kitchen faucet, and dried them. Kyle paused the TV. Jenna looked up from her homework.

"This is my election year. Someone is filing to run against me."

"Who?" asked Liz.

"A guy from the D.A.'s office. I'm going to win," I said with more confidence than my body's innards would have suggested actually existed. "Not many judges get challenged and, when they do, they usually win."

Kyle, perhaps allowing opportunism to mix freely with pragmatism, said, "Even if you stopped being a judge wouldn't you just go back to being an attorney and make more money than you make now?" His silver-lining laced comment provided a welcome contrast to the tenor of the conversations I'd had with my challenger in front of the courthouse and the reporter on the phone.

"True, but let's not start assuming anything. He hasn't filed his election papers yet." My breath was coming easier. "Right now,

I'm just going to start trying to gather some support. All the judges are behind me."

"We'll pray about it," Liz said.

Jenna went back to her homework, Kyle started a video game, and I went to the bedroom to change out of my work clothes. As I took off my tie, button down shirt, slacks, dress socks, and replaced them with jeans, T-shirt, pullover fleece and tube socks, the burden of the election challenge seemed slightly—the slightest slightly possible—to have lifted. Dinner, some television, bedtime, everything happened like it did any other night. We'll handle this, I thought. Which is why I was utterly unprepared for what happened the next morning.

The alarm went off at 4:15, like usual. Liz was already up and in the room down the hall doing some Bible study while I made the bed. She came in and we prepared to say prayers together, just like we do every morning before heading out to hit the gym. We knelt on opposite sides of the bed. If I had been asked about it, I'd have said up to that point that this was just another morning. Then I opened my mouth to pray.

"Father . . ."

And then nothing.

Silence.

My head dropped down between my arms, my forehead pushing into the comforter I'd just smoothed out across the mattress when making the bed.

Silence.

Nothing.

Then, something.

My shoulders shook. My lungs expanded with a huge in-draw of breath. And I cried. Not quietly crying tiny tears into the bed. Not quietly crying softly stifled whimpers.

Huge heaving sobs.

Huge heaving sobs that shook me from my knees on the floor, up through my belly and into my chest, up to my head and then down my arms as I pressed them into the bed. Uncontrollable crying. I don't mean I tried to control it but found I couldn't. I had no thought of control. My body was in charge, not my thinking.

I didn't hear Liz get up from her side of the bed. I didn't feel the mattress shift as she stopped leaning against it. I didn't know she was coming around to me.

The first I knew was when she knelt down and wrapped me up in her arms. Then she prayed.

"God, be with Tim," she began. Liz's words washed over me, her arms holding me, her prayer encouraging me. My sobs stopped. My breathing eased. She asked for God's presence to comfort me, strengthen me, calm me. Then she said, "Amen."

I stayed silent.

"Are you going to be all right, or should I stay home?"

"I'm fine." I lifted my head off the mattress. "Go ahead." I took a couple gulps of air. "I'm going to the gym, too."

"I think you should," she said. "It'll be good to work out. You need the endorphins."

Liz thinks most problems are helped by a good workout. She's not wrong. Going by her own experience, there's nothing like a twelve-mile run or a two-hour gym workout (or both, if she has her way) to get your mind in the right place. My own runs and workouts are half hers, but she was still right. I had to stay with the routine and get time in at they gym. This stress wasn't going to make itself go away.

What I should have realized is that I wasn't just dealing with a stressful time of life. This went well beyond stress. It was something I hadn't seen in almost three decades and even back then it passed so quickly I'd almost forgotten it had ever happened.

∾

My first panic attack came in algebra class. A college algebra final exam classroom to be exact. During the final exam.

I didn't want to take college algebra but since I flunked the subject in high school and I hoped to transfer from my junior college (that's what we called community colleges back then) to the University of California, I needed to pass algebra. High school algebra had slipped through my fingers. I got a C in my first semester and an incomplete for my second semester grade. That meant I had to make up the incomplete or it became an F. I never made up the incomplete. I got an F.

I flunked high school algebra.

College algebra turned out to be no more difficult than high school algebra but that's probably because they were teaching the same basic algebra my high school teacher tried to get me to understand. Now, either I had become much smarter in the few short intervening years or my college instructor was an easier grader. In any case, when midterm grades came out I got an A.

Woo-hoo, I must have become a math whiz!

I soon learned I was not a math whiz. The second half of the semester hit me like a freight train. I put in the time reading, practicing equations (and I still don't get why one of them is called quadratic), and preparing for quizzes, but this was nothing like the ease I had found in the first half of the semester. Finals week came and I put in even more time studying and practicing. That final push gave me some hope I could finish strong. It was ill-placed confidence.

We had two hours for the final exam. I sat down, placed my papers and pens on the small desktop—the kind of desk that's fixed to the chair so you can't adjust the height of either desk or chair—and waited for the proctor to hand out the exams. I looked the test paper over. It looked like what we'd been studying. So far, so good. The first half hour I moved from one problem to the next, hoping I was getting the questions right. The second half hour I sat frozen to my seat. My mind gave me no warning, my body showed no signs of oncoming stress.

I just froze.

Actually, it's not accurate to say I froze entirely. At first, and I don't know for how long, I can't say what I thought because I have no memory of it. Then, my mind raced with thoughts. The problem was the thoughts were not working on the problems on the page. My thoughts were yelling at me.

"Snap out of this, Tim!"

I've noticed I tend to address myself by name when I'm like this.

"Finish this test! Finish this test, Tim! Get to work! You have to finish this test! You have to finish the test! You have to finish! You have to!"

The yelling wasn't helping. It's a good thing it was in my head because if the words were also said aloud I think my classmates would have found them unhelpful, too.

"Get back to work, Tim! What are you waiting for? Now! Now! Now!"

Did I say this lasted for a half hour? I'm guessing. At some point the yelling stopped. I realized my breathing must have been speeding up as I sat there because now it was slowing. And while I knew it was slowing and deepening, I had no sense of how long it had been coming fast and shallow.

I loosened the grip on my pen, once again able to hold it loosely like a normal person holds a pen. The clock said I had less than an hour left. My paperwork sat there on my desk just as I'd left it. I read the next problem and tried to work it out, it and as many more as I could before the proctor called time. That proctor called time much too soon for me to finish.

My score on the final exam escapes me but it must have been horrible since when averaged against the A from my midterm grade I ended up with a C for the course. At least it wasn't an F, and as my son later assured me when he was in college, "Cs for degrees, Dad!"

I took the C and transferred to UC Santa Barbara, where I never had a panic attack.

Chapter 4

An Assault on
Lungs and Brain

I DIDN'T KNOW HOW much the stress of the election was hitting me until a few days after that early morning when I cried in Liz's arms as she prayed over me. Sure, I was having a little trouble sleeping and got distracted more easily than usual, but the sobbing morning was just that once. Who wouldn't be stressed out with work and family and now an election challenge thrown in?

I was sick by the end of that week. It started in my sinuses and then settled generally from my forehead to my chest. Achy, congested, coughing, sneezing—I had it all. It got worse each day and I spent the weekend on my back.

I went to bed Sunday evening and woke up just before midnight, my head throbbing. I'd left some medicine on the bedside table along with a bottle of water. Breaking open the individually wrapped capsules containing pseudoephedrine and ibuprofen, I swallowed them down my swollen throat and hoped for relief. As soon as I laid back down, I realized my mistake; I'd just taken a stimulant in the middle of the night. There was no more sleep for me that night and when Liz woke up at the normal time for prayers and going to the gym I told her I hadn't yet gone back to sleep and needed to see if I could drop off for at least a couple hours before work. She got up and followed the schedule while I stayed in bed.

Awake.

For another two hours.

Dawn finally came and I got up.

I had to go to work.

There was a trial starting that morning and no other judge available to take it. Somehow, I arrived at the courthouse shaven and looking halfway presentable. Time came for the attorneys and the defendant to appear in my courtroom and a miracle occurred. The trial got called off.

Both attorneys agreed there was more investigation needed and they wanted to pick a new date for trial. It didn't take much to convince me. After addressing the logistics, I told them that it worked out well for me as I'd been up since midnight and was heading back home for a sick day.

"Losing that kind of sleep isn't something you recover from with just one good night's rest," the prosecutor said.

"I hope you're feeling better soon," the defense attorney added. "Good thing the courthouse is closed tomorrow. It'll give you another day to rest."

The next day was February 12, Lincoln's birthday, a day the courts are always closed in California. I planned to take full advantage of it. Schools were still open, so Liz had work and Jenna had classes while I got to sleep in. Kyle had graduated half way through his senior year so even though he hadn't yet turned eighteen he too had the day off. Sort of. We relied on him to do a lot of the driving and errands, including taking his sister to and from school. That day I had another trip ready for him when he got back from his morning errand run.

"I got the smoothie you wanted," he said, leaving a 24-ounce cup on the coffee table next to me.

"Thanks." I was sprawled out on the couch with a load of pillows under my head and a heavy blanket spread out on top of me. "Don't get too comfortable. We're going out again soon."

"OK. Where?"

"I called the doctor. They've got a slot open this morning. I'd rather not have to drive."

"OK." So he drove me.

We have a good doctor. Very good. He stays up on medical research and nags us to stay current on our annual check-ups.

"I hear crackles," he said as he listened to my lungs through his stethoscope. "Pneumonia."

I believed him because, after all, he's a good doctor. Plus, I felt awful. Awful sick, awful tired, and awful stressed. I told him how awful. Or at least I thought I did.

"I'll call in an antibiotic to your pharmacy. You'll feel better in a couple days."

I doubt it, I wanted to tell him. There was something more than pneumonia wrong with me. I knew it. I just didn't know how to talk about it.

We stopped for the drugs on the way home, I took a dose, and I went to sleep. I'd never felt as tired as those three weeks I spent recovering from pneumonia. It keeps your lungs from filling with air, which means your blood stream is not filling with oxygen, which means your body is not getting the basic element it needs for survival, sapping your strength with each breath you take as you try to get what you can't. But lung crackling pneumonia was not my biggest problem. Or maybe it's best to say it was no more than tied for first place among my biggest problems.

Stress can reduce your immune system's ability to fight off infection. I figure that's what led to me having my one and only bout with pneumonia crop up during that election. Being sick can in turn worsen the effects of stress, leading to anxiety or depression or both. That's what was happening to me; I just didn't know it yet.

Despite the all-out fatigue from pneumonia, I still couldn't sleep through the night. I'd go to sleep at the usual time, but wake up after two, maybe three, hours. It became an unwelcome and inevitable nightly routine. Nightly. As in every single night. In bed by 9:00 to accommodate our early rising for prayers and the gym, but awake much too soon. And staying awake.

Awake with racing thoughts.

Rushing thoughts.

But not random thoughts.

They were always about one thing: someone wanted me to lose my job, and I didn't want to give it up and stop being a judge. Perseveration was my constant companion. *I like my job,* I'd say in my head a hundred times. *Why would someone want to take it away from me?* The darkened bedroom ceiling over my head never answered me.

I'd tell myself it wasn't going to happen. The odds were in my favor and my opponent wasn't the type to get a groundswell of support, I'd argue. I'd assure myself that I was going to win. But my brain and body both told me I was in danger, I was under threat, and there was nothing I could do to get away from that threat, that danger. In the choices of fight, flight, or freeze, these sleepless sessions of racing thoughts froze me every night.

Eyes wide open, I stared at the ceiling fan sitting motionless above me; my own breathing was shallow, almost painful, as I listened to the deep breathing from my wife lying next to me. And once I got through the rapidly repeating but oddly coherent thoughts about my job being threatened, I'd launch into the ones that turned to screaming: *Get a grip, Tim! Pull yourself together! You're going to be a wreck in the morning!*

In the morning? This would go on for so long that eventually I'd look at the clock and see there was no need to try to talk myself into sleeping. I had to get up anyway.

That meant prayer time with Liz. I could get through that. Then the gym. I went—once I'd recovered from pneumonia—because she was going to work out at her gym so I might as well get up and go to mine. Then back home for a shower and get to work. How could I do all that? I don't know. For some reason everything was easier in the morning—even after a sleepless night—than in the afternoon and evening. Those were always the worst. Tired and worn out from a long day at work, my body and my brain had both had enough by mid-afternoon.

Mornings were easier, except for eating. I was off my feed 24 hours a day. I could go through the motions but it didn't matter.

I'd pour a bowl of cereal, lift a spoonful to my mouth, and the rest would sit in the bowl while I stared at it on the table. I'd pack a lunch to take to work and let it sit uneaten, unable to follow my usual habit of grazing on it in bits and pieces during breaks throughout the court day.

And dinner? I finally stopped trying to eat a regular evening meal and told Liz that if I felt hungry I'd make some toast, but not to bother trying to accommodate me when it came to the rest of the family eating dinner. I'd just sit at the table with her and the kids.

Some days that's all I did, just sit there. I'd feel so stressed I couldn't even join in the conversation let alone join in the meal. So I'd try to listen without letting my mind get into the monologue loop I dealt with every night. It was Kyle who came up with the idea that I should find food alternatives. If I couldn't stomach my usual, he suggested, what could I eat? I experimented.

Chocolate milk.

Yogurt, sometimes with fruit and a spoonful of granola.

Smoothies.

Toast. I'd already discovered that one. I also discovered I could handle peanut butter and jelly on toast, so I ate that.

But I still wasn't eating much. My weight was dropping, and it wasn't just from battling pneumonia. I was so stressed that even sticking with the few foods I could eat wasn't enough. Thirty pounds not enough. That's how much weight I dropped overall during the election, and the weight loss didn't stop until the election was over. You'd have thought I'd be happy about losing weight. I've tended toward chunkiness most of my life.

～

"Aren't you the one they call Blimp?" some girls asked me in seventh grade. I ducked my head and moved down the hall. But it was true. A group of skinny guys had decided that me being a little thicker—not fat, but certainly not rail thin like they all were—meant that I was suitably nicknamed Blimp.

Going from five feet one inch as a freshman to five feet ten inches by the time I graduated high school did wonders for thinning me out, but growth spurts end and I continued eating like they didn't. The tendency toward chunkiness slowly returned. Keeping my weight down takes vigilance and I'm not always vigilant about what I eat.

So, you might have reasonably thought I'd welcome the stress-induced dieting. I didn't. I looked at food I knew I should want to eat. I'd look at pizza. I love pizza. I'd look at chili. I love chili. I'd look at pie. I love pie. The thought of eating any one of those made me sick to my stomach, which meant that I was really messed up. And I knew it.

∾

Liz saw the toll stress was taking, and I came to rely on her to be strong when I was at my weakest. Was I really at my weakest? I can't remember being weaker. I'd never felt so tired, exhausted, fatigue-ridden, absolutely physically spent as when fighting pneumonia. But it went further. My emotions, my intellect, every aspect of me felt emptied of the ability—even the desire—to go on.

Both work and home became harder. Once I realized Jenna and Kyle must be seeing it, I knew I needed help to handle what I couldn't handle on my own. I needed medical help. Our doctor is always checking email day and night, so a few days after the visit where he put me on the antibiotics with assurances that I'd feel better in a couple days, I wrote to tell him I wasn't. I described the nights wide awake, the distracted thinking, the loss of appetite, the load of stress pushing me down, and down, and down.

He emailed back and said his nurse would be expecting a call from me in the morning and he'd see me as soon as I could get in. I made the call and went in. I told him all the things I should have told him at the pneumonia appointment. All the things I should have but couldn't. It's hard to put into words the things you want someone else to just know, to take care of for you, without having to explain what's wrong.

Like how almost every waking moment is spent worrying about your future. Worry that isn't just "Gee, I hope everything turns out all right." Worry that is a constant, repeating round of

"My life is falling apart and every single thing about it is hard and I can't eat and I can't sleep and I don't know how to fix it and I can't stop thinking about it and why is my heart beating so fast and my emotions are right on the surface and about to tear through my skin in the middle of the courtroom or onto my kids and I just want everything to stop but it never stops!"

That kind of worry.

I figure the reason I could put it in words for him this time was because of the kids. Once I got the pneumonia diagnosis, I stayed home sick from work. Staying home sick from work meant I was around the house and that meant around my kids more every day. In my email to the doctor laying out what was going on and why I wanted to come back to see him again so soon, I wrote toward the end: "I'm afraid this will affect Kyle and Jenna. They must notice how I'm acting. How could they not?"

My concern for them forced me to write it all down in an email, and then to expand on it in the examination room. My doctor told me about stress and my body, about the effect stress has on the body's chemistry balances, and that my brain's activity was out of whack when it came to serotonin levels. It turns out serotonin is important. It should flow freely from one nerve to another in the brain. Mine didn't. Stress can tell your brain's nerve endings to grab back serotonin they just released so the next nerve in line cannot pick it up. It's called serotonin reuptake, and it's a bad thing. That's what mine did. My brain was reuptaking a lot.

There's medication for that and he prescribed some. The problem was that it doesn't take effect right away and it doesn't make all the symptoms completely disappear. "For that to happen," he said, "you'll have to stop being under stress. You've already got a stressful job."

"But I don't feel stressed about work," I said.

"I think you do, but you've gotten so used to it that you think the way you feel under the stress you face daily is normal. It's not, and this election has pushed you over the edge of what you can handle."

The phrase "generalized anxiety disorder" went into my chart, noted as being the result of stress. He wasn't going to give me any more of a diagnosis than necessary to justify the prescription. "You have symptoms of anxiety and depression both," he explained, "but I don't want to put 'depression' in your record."

"OK . . ." I wasn't following him.

"Your records are confidential, but you never know. Once the word 'depression' is written down it's there forever. The stigma attached to it is real for a lot of people and can affect how others choose to see you."

"You mean real for someone like me who's running for re-election, and for voters who are deciding whether to vote for me."

"Exactly. I describe the symptoms of my patients. I don't use the word 'depression' in the conclusions I draw from those symptoms unless it's medically necessary."

"And for me?"

"It's not medically necessary. You've got anxiety and you're experiencing depression. The treatment is the same. I don't have to write them both down."

I picked up the prescription on the way home, took a pill before I left the pharmacy's parking lot, and settled in for another afternoon of worsening symptoms.

Afternoons were always the worst.

Chapter 5

Law School, Lawyering, and the Fellowship of Judging

I COULDN'T HAVE BECOME a judge without first being an attorney, and before I became an attorney I spent three years studying law.

Law school was no stress.

Even getting into law school was no stress. I truly assumed that I would get in and that there was no reason I wouldn't graduate. Why no unbridled anxiety? Maybe because my track record led me to believe it. College, except for that one algebra final, always fell into place for me, from application to graduation.

During my senior year of high school, I thought I wanted to be a forest ranger so I applied to Humboldt State University's forestry major. I didn't know you were supposed to apply to more than one school so it was either Humboldt let me in or no one would. I got in. By the time I graduated high school I changed my mind and enrolled in junior college. I started thinking I wanted to be a history major and applied to transfer to UC Berkeley, although we called it Cal back then. I didn't know you were supposed to apply to more than one school, even when transferring from junior college. Cal's history major was considered an impacted program but I got in there, too. By the time I was supposed to transfer I changed my mind and wanted to major in environmental studies, so I stayed in junior college another semester and applied to UC Santa Barbara. I still didn't know you were supposed to apply to more than one school so either UCSB took me or I stayed yet another year in junior college. I got in. This time it stuck. I moved onto the UCSB campus and stayed for two and a half years.

With all the applications and acceptances and changes and maneuvering, it was going to take a combined total of a minimum of five years to finish college. I turned it into six after deciding at the last minute to defer graduation so I could spend a year studying abroad at the University of Sussex, nestled in a valley between the villages of Falmer and Stanmer outside of Brighton, England. Spending a year in England made applying for law school a challenge, but at least by then I knew you were supposed to apply to more than one school at a time. I still didn't know about safety schools, though. I just applied to universities that looked like they had good law schools in parts of the country I wouldn't mind living in for three years.

Being in England the year I was applying for law school also meant finding somewhere to take the Law School Admission Test. The LSAT is tightly controlled and closely proctored. In my home state of California it was offered a few times each year at dozens of sites. In England it was offered once a year and at only one site. I put in my paperwork to take the test in London. A few weeks later I received it back.

In pieces.

The multi-page (and now even more multiple-piece) application was in a clear plastic postal service wrapper with a printout notifying me the envelope got caught in the sorting machine, which machine then proceeded to rip it apart like a toddler teething on a picture book. The final line in the notification apologized for any inconvenience. Inconvenience? Either I took the London LSAT or I didn't go to law school the next year. Yes, I'd classify this as inconvenient.

One particular scrap in the collection of pieces encased in the plastic envelope was large enough to contain the address and telephone number of the London office handling the test arrangements. I went to the payphone outside my flat and dropped a shilling in the slot. Once I dialed the London number the operator came on and told me to drop more shillings. I did. Ring-ring.

"I tried to sign up for the LSAT but my paperwork was ruined in the mail."

"Oh, how terribly inconvenient," the test place woman told me in confirmation of the postal service's take on the matter. "Still, just come around our office and we'll set you right."

"I'm at university in Sussex," I explained, using British syntax to grease the communication along. My British friends called me a very switched-on Yank.

"We're open Saturdays until noon." She sounded quite cheery about working weekends.

That Saturday I took the earliest train from the village of Falmer to Brighton, where I transferred to the London Victoria train. Then I took the Tube across London and got off near Madame Tussauds. No time for the wax museum. I walked five long London blocks to a side street, turned right, found the first alley on the left, and saw the office sitting there on the corner.

The cheery woman was true to her word. She set me right and I was all signed up for the test scheduled for a month later. You would have thought I'd be stressing over this. No. I stayed calm, never breaking a sweat either literally or metaphorically. Mr. Cool, taking it all in easy loping strides.

The LSAT went fine. They administered it in the basement of a London social club, one of those places from a P.G. Wodehouse novel where octogenarians take naps in overstuffed leather wing-backed chairs while the younger set walk around with tennis rackets and talk about their polo ponies. The basement had neither wing-backed chairs nor polo ponies.

It did have a very pleasantly-voiced older woman as chief proctor for the test, reminding me of a favorite elementary school teacher but with an English accent. "Please do let me know if you need anything," she said as she smiled beatifically upon her test-taking brood.

By the end of the exam I was spent, but I must have spent wisely because when I got my test results a few weeks later it turned out I'd aced the LSAT.

Of the six law schools I sent my test results to (since, of course, everyone knows you're supposed to apply to more than one school at a time), five thought me good enough. I chose King Hall School of Law at UC Davis. The only thing I knew about the City of Davis was that it had a sign on an exit on the freeway between the Bay Area where I grew up and the state capital of Sacramento. The first time I set foot in that small college town was the day I moved into the grad student dorm.

The law school held a welcoming barbecue reception the Sunday night before orientation classes started. With hamburgers on the grill and cold beer in the keg, I thought I could have done worse in choosing schools. The next morning's first session of orientation week proved me right.

"Welcome to King Hall," the Director of Admissions said. "Look to your right and look to your left."

Uh-oh, I thought. I'd heard about this from friends who had gone to other law schools. This look-to-your-right-and-left drill was followed by "One of you won't be here by then end of the first year" as an apparent effort to motivate through fear. But I was wrong.

"Look to your right and look to your left," she said. "One of you is likely a returning student who has been out in the workplace for a few years since college. Another studied fine art or philosophy. And some of you are parents with small children. This year's class is a diverse collection of scholars."

Scholars? Me, a scholar? The Dean interrupted my thoughts as he took the podium.

"Welcome to King Hall," he said, in echo of the Admissions Director. "I'm going to mention something once and once only. Final exams come at the end of the term. You are not at the end of the term, so don't worry about them. Now that I'm done mentioning that, I have some good news for you. You all had what it takes to get into King Hall and you all have what it takes to graduate. And since you are all going to do well here and in your future careers, let me also encourage you to do good while you are at it."

Yes, I'd landed at the right school.

≈

Students I speak to—whether high school or college or in law school—often ask how to become a judge. Here's the secret: do the best you can to get good grades in high school so you can get into the best college for you; then do the same in college so you can get into the best law school possible; work well enough in law school to get a job with a good law firm or government agency, or to set up a successful practice on your own; then put in the work as an attorney so that you get a good reputation, a reputation good enough so that if you decide to apply for a judgeship there are people willing to speak up for you. Then it's up to the Governor to choose between you and everyone else who has put in the work over their careers, too.

What does all of this do for you as a judge? It prepares you to continue to put in the work. That leads to a good reputation as a judge. At least, you hope it does. I must have pulled it off well enough because my colleagues on the bench—both in my courthouse and around the state—came alongside me in the 2008 election almost without fail.

≈

Judges can't engage in politics. It's right there in the California Code of Judicial Ethics. That was no hardship for me. I wasn't political before taking the bench and having a state regulation that prohibits me from becoming political gives me cover when people running for office call and ask for an endorsement. Judges shouldn't be seen as endorsing a political party or a politician since local, state and federal officials are the ones that pass the laws that judges are sworn to apply without—among other things—regard to any connections the laws may have to political interests. But just because I hadn't a personal political history doesn't mean all judges have always been apolitical. Some have been very political before taking the bench, like my colleague Dave.

Dave was a political powerhouse. He graduated law school at U.C. Davis on the G.I. Bill in the 1970s and soon joined the Governor's office with a position on the Chief of Staff's team. When the governorship changed parties, he went into private practice and took on local politics: a City Council seat, then Mayor, then a spot on the county's Board of Supervisors, and eventually chair of that board. He'd kept his hand in statewide issues, too, so when his old boss the Chief of Staff ran for and became Governor, Dave was asked to join the team. From there he became a judge a few years later.

You might think Dave got the job because he's so politically connected. That's not incorrect, but it is misleading. Dave is an extremely hard worker who is also highly intelligent. Just like so many other judges, Dave put in the work to show how qualified he is for the bench. I was glad to welcome him in 2003 for those reasons, as well as the fact that Dave never met a committee he wouldn't want to serve on. As one of my fellow judges put it when Dave's appointment was announced, "I'll never have to say yes to another committee assignment now that Dave's here to take them."

In 2008 I found another reason to appreciate Dave's presence on our local bench. As soon as my opponent announced his intention to run against me, Dave sat me down. "We are going to beat this guy. I've already started drafting an email I'll send out tonight to my contacts on my home email to line up endorsements for you. We're going to overwhelm Walker in this campaign."

We.

Dave said "we" and my heart raced. Not stress-induced racing this time. Dave was committing to me, and that meant that Dave's well-honed political prowess—there wasn't any other word for it—was going to be working for me in the one type of election campaign the Code of Judicial Ethics allows—a judicial election. No sitting on the sidelines or half-hearted support. Dave committed to coming alongside me for the duration of the campaign. From that point until the results came in on Election Night I had the most powerful and effective former political operative in the county on my team.

He wasn't afraid to make me face the truth, either, like when he said early on, "You know you brought this on yourself."

I did know it. I knew my history on the bench.

$\sim$

One drawback of being named to the bench so young is the lack of seasoning that comes with age and experience. At 35, I wasn't the youngest person ever to become a judge in California but I was decidedly on the young side by about a decade if you look at the average age of judicial appointment. It showed in my early years on the bench. Not that my rulings were unsound; I was rarely taken up on appeal and when it did happen I was much more likely to be affirmed than reversed. Reversals are rare for trial court judges.

No, my deficit was in my demeanor. I ran a tight courtroom and anytime it looked like there was something—or someone—slipping out from my control I got agitated. Sometimes very agitated, especially in the earliest years, and it showed. Rather than display the dignified patience you expect from a judge, I'd speak sharply and loudly, telling an attorney to sit down or a litigant to stop talking. I'd never use the words "shut up" or yell at someone "Get out of my courtroom" but a judge doesn't have to go to those extremes to cross the line of judicial demeanor. When you're the person in the black robe sitting on a bench elevated above everyone else in the room, your words get magnified.

For example, if I were quiet, calm, and said in a flat tone, "Counsel, I thought you told me your paperwork would be in by now. How much more time do you think you need?" someone walking out of the courtroom later might remark, "Did you hear how upset the judge was with that lawyer?" And then perhaps if at the next hearing I said, "Counsel, this is your third chance to get your motion heard and you still haven't filed your briefs. You've had all the chances I'm going to give you. The motion is dropped," someone might possibly say, "The judge almost held that attorney in contempt!" A raised voice isn't required for the judge's words to be construed as forceful, and, frankly, a judge's words are supposed to carry force. But when a judge adds in that raised voice, the effect is enhanced inordinately. We have a name for judges who habitually indulge themselves in raising their voices in order to bully people in the courtroom. We call them Robe Heavy; they wear their robes like a weapon and wield it on the hapless attorneys, litigants, witnesses and jurors appearing before the judge.

I don't think I made a habit of bullying from the bench, but on occasion in the early years I did speak sharply when—in retrospect—I now realize a soft voice would have sufficed. After all, "A gentle answer turns away wrath, but a harsh word stirs up anger," as it says in Proverbs 15.

By 2008, I'd matured into the job quite a bit. The problem was that my opponent could call upon instances of being in my courtroom in those early years that he could personally attest to. Happily, as my colleague Dave assured me after pointing out this election challenge was my own fault, "Once he brings this up, all people are going to hear is that you keep lawyers in line." For most voters, a judge who's hard on lawyers must be a good judge so I figured that campaign strategy wasn't going to get him far.

Dave's offer of help paid off immediately. When I awoke the next morning and checked my personal email, I saw Dave had forwarded dozens of endorsements from local civic leaders. The same thing happened the next morning, and the next, and the next. Every day for weeks the endorsements rolled in. Maybe this was one of the reasons mornings were easier for me, even if I had spent the night staring at the ceiling trying to quiet my brain from the racing thoughts of how awful I felt emotionally and physically. Good news has a way of tamping down stress, which in turn tamps down anxiety.

Other judges came alongside as well. Kathy, an extravert and a superb logician, told me, "On election night you're going to need a place to celebrate. Have your party at my house. I'll take care of it." Her confidence and kindness repeated throughout the campaign, and she was a constant voice of inevitable success even though

I might have my own doubts during the ensuing months. Arvid gave me permission to walk into his chambers at any moment, and if I said "I need to hear something positive right this minute" he promised to drop whatever he was doing, sit me down, and then make sure I didn't leave his office until I was filled to buoyancy with encouraging words. All the judges in the courthouse came alongside me one way or another. Having friends and colleagues come alongside with extremely able assistance took me back to one of my earliest memories.

~

When I was a four-year-old, we visited some friends who had a swimming pool. My Dad was in the water with me for a while, and some older kids—all teenagers—had taken turns with me as well. After a while everyone got out, with the grownups gathering around the grill to visit with one another as they cooked dinner. Me? I wandered away from that group and found myself back at the pool's edge.

Then I stepped in.

Splash!

Down I went like a box of rocks, but soon felt myself gripped by the arm and drawn back up to the surface where Dad unceremoniously plopped me on the pool deck.

"What were you doing?" he asked.

"You guys were supposed to watch me."

I know the dialog is accurate because my Dad got a lot of mileage out of that story over the years.

~

I got a lot of mileage out of my colleagues' help during the campaign, too, but sometimes the offers of help misfired. One Friday in the first half of the campaign season, I'd made it through the day fairly unscathed by the usual burgeoning anxiety, the voice in my head that drowned out everything but the thoughts of being overwhelmed, the physical manifestations of racing heart and shallow breath—all of which for some reason that particular Friday afternoon were well below the surface rather than threatening to expand and leak through my skin. I looked at the clock, saw it had reached 5:00, and thought I might make it home without an anxiety attack—or near attack—for the first time in a long while. Then Steve walked in.

"I have a dinner meeting with some attorneys and judges in Sacramento tonight. You should come."

Steve, a newer judge but a little bit older than me, is tall and broad-shouldered and not quiet of voice. My office was small and I sat at my desk looking up at him filling half the room. His offer—more a pronouncement—came without preamble, no how-you-doing or are-you-free-tonight. I'm not one for spontaneity or group gatherings in the best of times. My body reacted to Steve before my brain processed what he said.

Racing heart.

Short breath.

Feeling about to crawl out of my skin.

My brain soon caught up. *Stop it! Why are you asking this? Just leave, please . . . leave. I just want everything to stop!* Not that I said any of this out loud.

"Not tonight, but thanks," is what I said out loud. "I'm going to go home and have dinner with the family." I thought that would be the end of it.

It wasn't.

"I figured this would give you a chance to get some more support from people over in Sacramento," he went on. "This is a good group for you to meet."

Why does he keep talking? I said in my head. *What do I have to do to make him stop? Why is my chest feeling so tight? I'm breathing hard, aren't I? Can he see me breathing hard? I hope he can't see me breathing hard.*

"Thanks," I said so he could hear. "I've got a plan for going to meetings and tonight isn't part of it. I'm going to stick with the plan." I didn't really have a plan for that night except the plan to go home and hide.

"OK," Steve said. "I just thought it was a good idea." He was still talking! But then he turned to the door and said, "Have a good weekend."

Up until the moment he walked in my door I thought the weekend was off to a great start. Now it looked like I'd barely make it home.

That's the thing about anxiety. It takes reasonable events and turns them into scenes from a horror novel. Consider Steve's offer: it was a great suggestion, and looking back on it I can understand why he might have thought I was nuts to pass it up. In a sense I was nuts, in that my brain was not processing his offer with anything remotely approaching a reasonable thought process. If anyone running for judge were to ask me if they should take an offer like Steve's, I'd tell them to jump at it.

∾

That Friday afternoon conversation might have been a misstep for me, but Steve came through in a big way on something that could have taxed my strength in both body and mind throughout the campaign: the judges' on-call schedule.

Police officers and Sheriff's deputies and child welfare workers and probation officers pull graveyard shifts as a matter of course. Judges do not. My day at the courthouse usually starts by 7:30 every morning and I leave around 5:00 for the evening. If someone needs to submit a search warrant request for a judge's review during the day, the clerks at the main desk downstairs find a judge who's not on the bench at the moment and send the officer along to chambers.

What happens when court is closed and there's no clerk to direct the officer or social worker to a judge's office? We get called at home. Dinner time, weekends, and the middle of the night are all fair game. To spread out the work we take the on-call duty a week at a time, which means each judge covers the after-hours calls about five weeks in a year.

Typically, the phone rings, wakes me, and I roll out of bed to pick it up. Sometimes my wife beats me to the phone and hands it to me saying, "It's a detective for you." Or it could be a patrol officer or a child welfare social worker. They might ask for an emergency protective order in a domestic violence case, a search warrant for a midnight homicide investigation, or a bail enhancement on a case that falls outside the standard bail amounts usually imposed. These are a few examples, but there are more types of requests than I would ever have imagined before becoming a judge. I always have to wake up enough to understand the request and decide whether to approve it, but I've learned not wake up so much that I can't go back to sleep after I hang up. These middle of the night phone calls may be part of the officer's regular shift but I still need my rest to be ready for court the next morning. It's hard enough to go back to sleep after one phone call, then another, then a third. At that point sleep is not just elusive. It's almost always impossible. (As I write this, I recall that just last Friday I was the on-call judge and the phone rang four times between the time I went to bed and the pre-dawn hours of Saturday morning. Saturdays are the days I don't get up before daybreak to say prayers with my wife and get to the gym. I got up before daybreak last Saturday.)

Soon after I got the pneumonia diagnosis I was supposed to be on-call. It's not impossible to handle the duty when you're at home feeling sick. I'd done that before, but not when I was sick with something as serious as pneumonia plus the constant stress and almost as constant anxiety and at times debilitating depression. That's when Steve jumped in.

"You're on-call next week," he said, voice carrying over the phone and bouncing off the walls of my house. He was at work. I was at home splayed out on the couch.

"I know. I should be able to handle it." I wasn't actually sure I'd be able to handle it, but I didn't want to admit that.

"I'm going to take it," he said.

"Do you want to swap weeks?" I asked. We did that at our courthouse, trading on-call weeks when they fell on a planned vacation or during an education conference.

"No," Steve said. "I'm just taking it. You get better."

His gesture—no, it was more than a mere gesture—his selfless willingness to take that load off me lightened my heart. I tried to say thanks but my emotions were already close to the surface that afternoon and his consideration and kindness made my voice catch in my throat like a sob. I covered it by coughing, then bought some more time by following the cough with moderate throat clearing.

When I trusted my voice again I said, "This'll help. I'm not getting much rest. I might be off another week, maybe two, but then I can get back to work."

"I checked. Your next on-call week is the end of April." That was a little more than two months away.

"I can cover it by then."

"No. I'm going to take that one, too. You've got a campaign to run. Don't worry about on-call weeks until after June 3."

June 3, 2008, was Election Day. Steve was taking my on-call duties, midnight phone calls and all, taking all of the work and all the sleeplessness, he was taking all that off of me and onto himself, adding it to his own already scheduled on-call weeks.

Big Steve, with his broad shoulders and loud, reassuring voice, carried my load.

∼

Sometimes middle of the night phone calls come in asking *me* to carry someone else's load, like when I awoke to the phone's ring a couple years before that election.

It was a few minutes after 1:00 on a Sunday morning, rousing me from a very deep sleep. Liz made it to the phone before I did, then handed it over to me and said, "It's Glen."

But I don't know any cops named Glen, I thought as I put the phone to my ear. It wasn't a cop. It was the senior pastor of our church. He wanted to know if I could preach that morning. Just past 1:00 on a Sunday morning and the first of two morning services was less than eight hours away.

I said yes.

Why? Because back in 2006 I used to write Bible studies for our church every week. They were always on the passage being preached on Sunday and were then printed on the reverse of the sermon notes included in that week's bulletin. The study took the reader through six days of in-depth exploration of the theme of the sermon. This was one of the reasons Glen called me; he knew I'd written the Bible study on the passage for that Sunday's sermon.

The other reason he called me was because he was in the emergency room in excruciating pain and about to go into the operating room for an unplanned gall bladder surgery.

So, I said yes. As I hung up the phone, I knew the first thing I had to do was try to fall back to sleep for at least a short while if I was going to be preaching two services in the morning. I could set my alarm to get up early enough to craft the Bible study I wrote into sermon format, I thought.

It was a good thought and, acting upon it, I tucked my body back under the covers where I promptly proceeded to lie awake for two hours thinking about all I needed to do to get ready to preach. I finally dropped off around 3:00, woke up to the alarm I'd reset for 5:00, got to work on the sermon itself, arrived at church by 8:00, and drank sufficient coffee to stay awake long enough to get behind the pulpit for both services. Apparently, I spoke coherently since the church posted the audio of the sermon to the church archives on its website.

Whether it's me carrying the preaching load for Glen calling from the ER, or Steve carrying the on-call load for me through my campaign, God gives us strength directly as well as by strengthening those he places around us. Still, the burden of life can crush, as I learned in that campaign season. But then I find words like this:

"Come to me, all you who are weary and burdened, and I will give you rest. Take my yoke upon you and learn from me, for I am gentle and humble in heart, and you will find rest for your souls. For my yoke is easy and my burden is light" (Jesus, in Matthew 11). This is a passage that, even when I am wearied with burdens that lead me to feel anxious, worried, afraid, and confused, gives me hope.

Why hope? Because Jesus says that no matter what I'm dealing with, he is not going to make it any harder. In fact, he says he'll make it easier than it would be without him by my side. I've learned to trust him on this. Sometimes I am alone and he comes alongside me and settles my mind. Sometimes he brings people to come alongside and prop me up. Either way, it is a fulfillment of this principle:

"Praise be to the God and Father of our Lord Jesus Christ, the Father of compassion and the God of all comfort, who comforts us in all our troubles, so that we can comfort those in any trouble with the comfort we ourselves receive from God" (2 Cor 1:3-4).

God comforts, and leads people to comfort those around them. He does this by coming alongside us, and by bringing people to come alongside us as well. This is literally what the word translated "comfort" in this passage means. It's from the same word used to describe the Holy Spirit, the Counselor, who is the one who comes alongside us. This passage in 2 Corinthians might be translated as praise for "the God of all coming-alongsidedness, who comes alongside us in all our troubles, so that we can come alongside those in any trouble with the coming-alongsidedness we ourselves receive from God." God's comfort is delivered to us as he comes alongside us, and our comfort—received and given—is found when we are alongside those God has put in our lives.

Which brings me to how the people at church helped—or didn't—with my election challenge.

Chapter 6

Church

THIS REELECTION CAMPAIGN AROSE during my third stint on the church Elder Board. That call from Lauren at the newspaper came shortly before the next meeting of the board, and when I told the other board members—two pastors and a handful of lay people— they were sympathetic. Not that they understood, but they said encouraging things. All I remember, other than their vague offers of support, was that I was totally distracted from whatever church business was on the agenda that night.

Scott, one of the pastors, is my age. He and Kim went to college with my wife. Our older kids—our son and their daughter—were born ten days apart. We went through childbirth classes together, complete with stops for frozen yogurt after every class. Our families vacationed together when all the kids were young. Of the board members Scott knew me best, and was the one who got how hard this was. This is the guy who when I was going through another crisis once offered to cancel a vacation he was about to leave on. "Do you want me to stay here with you?" he asked.

That is the kind of friend Scott is to me. When it came to this campaign, Scott was a brick, checking in on me and praying with me and for me throughout. He had the coming-alongside-comforter thing nailed, and I was blessed by all he did.

Others weren't so good at being supportive.

"How's it going with the campaign?" one person asked at church soon after my doctor put me on the anti-anxiety meds.

"It's killing me." I'm not sure I said those words as much as choked them out.

"You can't say that!" He looked shocked. "Don't let anyone know. You need to present yourself positively confident one hundred percent of the time."

"Yeah," I said. "Um, thanks." I felt chastised, which I think was his intent.

We'd arrived at church early that morning and I looked around the courtyard hoping someone else would walk by, anyone I could go to, any way I could escape the crushing weight he'd just dropped onto my shoulders.

No one.

Thinking back now, I realize Scott would have been in his office. I could have gone there. Or I could have gone inside to find Liz where she'd probably be talking to a friend. But here's the thing about anxiety and depression. It doesn't equip you to help yourself and it doesn't equip you to seek out help. When anxiety hits, the only thing you want is for it to stop. No one walked across the courtyard to make it stop. Eventually, I drifted inside.

Months later, after the campaign, after reflecting on my mental health battles, Liz and I talked about some of the events like that interchange in the church courtyard.

"You've got insights now that you didn't have before the election," she said. "Maybe you'll understand better when you deal with some of the people in your courtroom who are suffering as well." She didn't mean it as a criticism. She meant that I was now equipped in a way I hadn't been before. She was right.

I look back on that church courtyard conversation and wonder at how unsafe a place like church can be. I was standing in front of my church, a person asked how the campaign was going, and I said it was killing me. If I can't have that conversation safely with someone at church, where can I have it? It taught me something about myself, too, and I think it applies to others whose anxiety hits them the way mine hit me. A person who says they're hurting—like I did—is a person who might be open to accepting help.

What would have helped?

Words like "I'm sorry to hear that. What can I do?" Or perhaps "Things are that bad? Do you want me to pray for you right now?" Or (and this is a good one) "I can't imagine what you're going through, but I promise that if you tell me what's going on I'll listen to you and do my best to understand."

These are words I did hear from some people during the campaign, people who knew I was hurt and needed healing, some of whom were not fellow Christians but whom God brought alongside me to bring comfort and salve to my soul, people who carried me when I couldn't carry on. I've learned these are words I can say to the hurting people around me, too.

Liz was right. That's at least one thing I learned from my campaign against stress, anxiety, and depression.

$$\sim$$

Glen, the senior pastor, did not get off to a good start in supporting me. Early on, when he asked how I was and I said I was stressed, he said, "I can see that. What I don't understand is why. There's no way you're going to lose the election, is there?"

"I could lose. Some judges do."

"Do you need help?"

Now that sounded promising, so I said, "I'm going to need campaign contributions and endorsements to get votes."

"I don't endorse people," he said. "I did once but I got burned."

I knew what Glen was talking about. A few years before my reelection campaign a member of our church who was a county official ran for reelection and Glen endorsed her. Then a religious fringe group that opposed her politics discovered she was a member of our church and decided to picket us on Sunday mornings. It was on the local news, so the group showed up again the following Sunday and the one after that. This lasted a month until they found another cause to protest. We never saw them again but Glen still

felt burned by endorsing someone whose policies brought contro-
versy to the church.

"I get it," I said. "I might talk to Pat about supporting me." Pat
is married to Glen.

"Absolutely."

Pat said yes and I listed her on my endorsements. If that were
the end of the matter with Glen, I'd say he did what he could with
what he felt comfortable doing and, in that regard, would be no
different from others who might have good reason for staying out
of the campaign. But that wasn't the end of the matter.

A couple weeks later I was at church talking to some friends
before the service started, another courtyard conversation. Colleen and Tom's son and my son Kyle went to school together from
kindergarten through high school, and before the school years
they played on the same T-ball team. Colleen was their coach and
I was her assistant. When I asked them at church if they'd endorse
me in the election, it was no surprise they said yes and at the same
time told me they'd help out with lawn signs.

Glen must have overheard our conversation. As Colleen and
Tom walked up the church steps I heard him say, "A political endorsement, huh? Boy, I'll never do that again." He then launched
into his story about the county official and the protestors, ending
with "It's just not worth it."

"Well, that's certainly interesting," Tom said. He's a master at
dry commentary. They went inside.

I felt my heart beating faster and a pounding in my ears, but
it wasn't from mounting anxiety. This time the speeding heart
rate was based on pure rage, and this pounding in my ears was
the seething anger I found myself directing at Glen. What was he
thinking, telling stories like that? Who did he think he was to discourage people who just finished saying they were going to help
me? In fact, I thought, why didn't he just shut up?

The best thing that happened in that moment was the courtyard filled with people streaming from the parking lot to the church
steps, blocking my direct path to Glen. Some stopped to talk to me
while others shook Glen's outstretched hand as he greeted them.

After a couple brief conversations, I looked to the top of the steps. Glen was gone. He probably went inside for the start of the service.

By the time the service ended I no longer seethed. Anxiety took its place. Then again, that's what usually happened at church. I'd feel more anxious after the service was over than before it started. My mind took the time in the services to dwell on the election and it was too easy to get distracted, especially during the quieter moments of prayer or the sermon, and instead focus my thoughts of the challenges I faced every day. I can't remember what Glen preached on that day, but I do remember the anger was gone. It had tempered into resentment, which was always a perfect accompaniment for my anxiety. Like mushrooms with steak, but not as tasty.

At the end of the morning I saw Glen standing off a bit by himself. I walked over. Had God kept people away from Glen so I could approach? Did God give me a desire to go over to him, a desire strong enough to overcome the anxiety that typically made me want to find seclusion in the car as I waited for Liz and the kids to be ready to go?

"Glen, I get that you don't want to endorse people," I said without warm-up.

He started to respond. I plowed on.

"But you don't have to tell my supporters that endorsing me is a big mistake. Colleen and Tom had just told me they'd help on my campaign and then you come along and discourage them from doing any such thing."

"I didn't mean it that way."

"I know. I'd appreciate it if you didn't tell that story to anyone again until after the election." I walked to the car and found Liz waiting.

"I saw you talking to Glen," she said. "How'd that conversation go?"

"I don't know."

Later—maybe the next Sunday or the one after that—Glen stopped me after church as I was walking to the car. "Go ahead and put me down as a supporter," he said.

"You sure?" I wanted to say no thanks, you can keep your endorsement, but the words that came out were "You sure?"

"Yes." He looked uncomfortable. "Pat and I are both supporting you."

I already knew I had Pat's endorsement but didn't point that out.

"OK. Thanks."

Relief flowed across his face. Glen hates it when he thinks people are mad at him. "Whatever you need, just let us know."

"Will do." I caught up with Liz.

"What was that about?" she asked.

"He's endorsing me now.

"What changed his mind?"

"He didn't say. Maybe Pat?"

"How do you feel about that?"

"It's fine," I said. "He's just trying to do the right thing."

And aren't we all, I thought.

～

Other people at church offered to help as well: endorsements, lawn signs, or contributions, and sometimes all three. One member, Paul, came through with unusually specific assistance when he approached me in the courtyard the Sunday after the story broke in the newspaper.

"Do you want to win this race?"

"Absolutely." What an odd question, I thought.

"You need a good campaign manager. Do you have one?"

"No. I've kind of been looking." Which really meant I'd kind of been avoiding it because thinking about hiring anyone made me think of all the work I was facing, and thinking of all the work I was facing stressed me out, and getting more stressed brought my anxiety to the surface. Campaign thoughts filled me with resentment that someone wanted my job, resentment at now having to fight to hold onto my job, resentment that I might lose my job, and resentment that my opponent—who was completely unqualified to be a judge—thought himself better at my job than me and who did he think he was anyway? Paul cut through my brain chatter.

"Call my friend, Chris. He's really good, very nice, and will work hard." He gave me Chris's number.

"Thanks," I said. "When should I call him?"

"Today."

Chapter 7

Campaign

I CALLED CHRIS.

"Paul told me he'd give you my number," Chris said, "but I think it's too early to start anything formal right now. The filing period hasn't even closed. You'll be fine waiting until then. How about we meet for lunch after that?"

He was right. Walker, my opponent, had announced his candidacy and issued a press release but he hadn't submitted his final paperwork to the elections office. Chris' assurance in that phone call that we could handle things as they come was in marked contrast to conversations I had with other potential campaign managers along the way.

The first conversation was with someone I didn't even realize was auditioning for the campaign manager job. All I knew was that a lawyer in town offered to introduce me to a friend who might be able to help my campaign. I met him. We talked. I can't tell you anything he said except that he told me he probably wouldn't be able to work on my campaign full time. *Why would I expect him to work on it full time? I barely know the guy*, I thought. I thanked him and my friend the lawyer, got up from the restaurant breakfast I'd kind of pushed around on my plate, and drove in to work. The meeting felt as empty of substance as my morning appetite.

I told Liz about it over the phone.

"That's weird," she said, which is a common way for Liz to summarize anything that doesn't square up. "Why'd they bother meeting with you?"

"No clue." With that, I put it out of my mind.

When I got home from work that night there was a folder waiting at my front door, the kind used for business presentations.

"While unable to represent you full time," the cover sheet read, "I have put together a proposal of steps to take on your behalf along with a pricing schedule." It was from my erstwhile breakfast date.

The following pages listed tasks he would perform, from immediately reserving space on campaign mailers, to purchasing lawn signs, to helping draft my candidate's statement for the official voters' pamphlet. All could be mine for a mere few thousand dollars. That is, his fee was a few thousand dollars. The cost of the campaign mailers, lawn signs, and candidate statement filing fee were not included. The more I read, the more my stress level rose. This was a minimal amount of work? What would a full campaign look like? And how was I supposed to handle it if he wasn't available to manage the campaign for me? Why did I have to see this in the afternoon? Afternoons were always the hardest.

My mind clouded over as I handed the folder to Liz.

"This is overwhelming," she said. "Did he tell you he was going to drop off a proposal?"

"No. I just thought he was a friend of a friend who could give me some advice and maybe volunteer for the campaign. I didn't know he did this for a living."

"What are you going to do?"

"Nothing."

"Nothing?"

"Not right now." I headed toward the bedroom to change.

Nothing ended up being exactly what I did with that proposal. I didn't even bother to call him to say thanks but no thanks. Avoiding things I didn't absolutely have to do, especially things that spiked my anxiety, was one of my go-to coping mechanisms.

Interviewing potential campaign mangers went downhill from there.

I called one guy whose first words when I told him I was being challenged for reelection were, "Why? What did you do wrong?"

"Uh, I don't . . . nothing."

"He must have picked you for a reason." His tone was accusatory, not curious.

"I don't know."

"Right," he said. "Look, I can probably help you. What do you want to do?"

"Can I get back to you?" I didn't get back to him.

Then there was the one who had managed successful campaigns for decades, both judicial and partisan, local and statewide, and who owned a high-powered public relations and lobbying firm. I met him in his large suite of offices near the state Capitol building. He came strongly recommended and confidence covered him like the posters from past campaigns covered his conference room walls. He represented a lot of local and statewide candidates and I assumed those that made the wall of the conference room were the successful ones. I was impressed with all his talk of accomplishing this and organizing that for me.

Until he asked my opinion on opposition research.

"How do you want to handle it if we turn up something on your opponent?"

"Turn up something? Like what?"

"Oh, I don't know . . . ." He was trying to sound off-hand. "Maybe something like a DUI, let's say."

"We'd never use it," I blurted out.

"Right, right." The back-pedaling in his thought processes raced across his face. "Of course. I just wanted to make sure we were on the same page."

Later over dinner that night I told Liz about the DUI question.

"Was he serious?"

"Completely."

"You can't hire him."

"Not planning on it."

Then I had that phone call with Chris, whose whole message was: "No problem. Plenty of time to run a campaign. Let's see how this plays out for now."

So I did. And when I eventually hired Chris and told him the one campaign manager's DUI question all he said was, "That's not a good way to win an election."

I'd chosen well.

~

As I said, California's Code of Judicial Ethics prohibits political activity. Judges can't endorse anyone, contribute more than a nominal amount, or engage in any partisan or even non-partisan political campaigns. California also considers judges elected officials, even if most judges are appointed rather than elected to office, never face an election challenge, and are merely declared the winner every six years for a new term. This pattern repeats itself until retirement.

The Federal courts and a few states have no judicial elections at all. Judges are appointed for life and keep judging until retirement. Still more states not only require elections but consider judgeships to be partisan political offices; politicking in its most familiar (and sometimes very ugly) partisan form is not only expected but required if you want to win.

California takes a middle ground. Judges can never be partisan, but they can campaign in a non-partisan way for their own re-election or to support someone else (whether a judge or attorney) in another judicial campaign. If the people of this state don't want judges to run a campaign, including all that goes with it such as gathering endorsements and collecting contributions, they could amend California's constitution to keep judges from being challenged at an election after appointment. As long as we can be challenged like other office holders, we have to be allowed to mount reelection campaigns to keep our jobs.

Some of the people I spoke to early on wanted to contribute financially. For that I needed to set up a campaign fund bank account and register it with the state's Fair Political Practices

Commission. I hadn't a clue how. My colleague Dave did. This is one great benefit of having a member of your court who'd been an extremely skilled politician in his previous life.

"You need a treasurer," he said.

"OK, but how do I find one?"

"You don't. You use mine." Dave had been quite successful in fund raising for years before taking the bench. "Call Vic," he told me as he wrote down the number for me.

I called Vic, a local CPA.

"I'll set it up," he said. "I just need a small amount to deposit to open the account. Usually $20 will do it."

I wrote a check for twenty dollars made out to the Committee to Reelect Tim Fall for Vic to deposit. I told Liz I was going over to his office to sign the bank paperwork and campaign finance registration forms.

"Ask him if his daughter goes to BSF."

Vic said she did. Liz had been in leadership with Bible Study Fellowship in our town and Vic's daughter was a regular. Vic and I started talking about our faith and then ran names by each other. That conversation could have been a stress test what with being forced to talk about money and fill out government forms, especially as it was yet another meeting smack in the middle of the afternoon. Afternoons were always the worst.

But we talked of faith and family and friends, and Vic told me that when it came to raising campaign money, I'd see the balance rise before I knew it. On top of being a full-time CPA, Vic had served as treasurer on local campaigns for years. If the money guy said not to worry about funds, who was I to argue? I went home calmer than I'd felt in weeks.

～

More support came from fellow judges, and not just the ones in my own courthouse. Judges from up and down California offered endorsements and wrote checks. It was a by-product of more than a decade of judicial branch committee work by then, and from teaching judicial education statewide over the years.

The year of the election challenge was also my first year serving on a new committee assignment, the California Judges Association Executive Board. My service on the CJA board must not have alienated anyone because every single one of the twenty-two members of the board pledged their support. They wrote checks for my campaign's bank account, gave me their names for my endorsement list, and some said they'd fly up on weekends to knock on doors if I needed help canvassing neighborhoods for the campaign.

I'd also been on the CJA ethics committee for about seven years by then. The committee members first learned of my challenge a few days after that initial phone call from Lauren, the reporter. Like the Executive Board, this group of judges from around the state pledged their names, their money, and their time. Plus, two of them had even more to offer: personal experience.

Kevin from San Diego took me aside at one of our meeting breaks that Saturday.

"The same thing happened to me a couple years ago. An attorney who had zero chance of ever getting an application through the Governor's office decided to take a run at me. Campaigning to keep your seat is a pain but you have to do it."

"That's my plan." I heard my words. They were coming across more confident than I felt. This was still in the very early days before I knew that what I was experiencing in my mind and body was the stress overtaking me both mentally and physically. It was before the pneumonia took hold and knocked me flat.

"I'm going to tell you something," Kevin said, "and you're not going to believe me."

I looked up at him expectantly. Not that I was sitting down while he stood next to my chair. We were both standing by the coffee and snack table. But Kevin stands well over six feet and I don't, so I looked up at him. Expectantly.

"Running for reelection will mean doing things you'd rather not. You'll have to go to events and ask people for money. Doing that will be a blessing in disguise."

My face must have betrayed my skepticism.

"Because of these campaign events you will get to meet people you'd never have met otherwise, good people who will make your life better. Other people are going to seek you out to offer help or to send money, and you'll be encouraged. It's hard to imagine this right now, but when it's all over you'll see it's true." I gave Kevin a weak smile and said thanks as the meeting started up again.

Ned from Santa Clara was the other committee member with personal experience. He'd been appointed to the Municipal Court and a few years later ran for an open seat on the Superior Court. We sat across from each other at a nearby coffee shop after the ethics meeting.

"First, you need to remember one thing. You are going to win this election."

"I hope so."

"No. Listen again. You are going to win. You've got work to do, and we'll go over that in a minute, but you are going to win."

He then gave me about five bullet points, including hiring a campaign manager and getting a treasurer. I was still weeks away from dealing with that, as it turned out, but how was I to know? I wrote down the bullet points.

"And finally, when you draft your ballot statement for the voters' pamphlet with all the reasons people should vote for you, remember that you have the number one best job title to put after your name: Superior Court Judge."

"Great." I wrote it down, pumped up.

"Your opponent has the second-best job title: Prosecutor."

"Oh," I said, deflated.

"His title only works when you're running against people who aren't judges or fellow prosecutors. You're a judge. Your job title's better."

Inflated again, I drove the ninety minutes home more encouraged than I'd felt on the morning drive down to the meeting. My colleagues are great.

The CJA Executive Board's judges were just as encouraging, pledging their support through the end of the election. We met for association business every other month, and I recall one meeting in the middle of the campaign vividly. CJA is a private professional association, so we typically met on weekends in windowless airport hotel conference rooms rented for the day, with the members driving or flying in for the meeting on a Saturday morning and returning home that evening. This particular meeting was in a better venue than most, being held in San Francisco's Ferry Building on the Embarcadero at the foot of Market Street. Twenty or so members were there with a long agenda ahead of us. We hunkered down, listened to reports, cast votes, ate box lunches of mediocre sandwiches, more reports, more votes, and by late afternoon there was only one item left: For the Good of the Order.

For the Good of the Order was our fancy way of asking if anyone wanted to talk about something not on the agenda. It might be judicial business or it might be the announcement of a new grandchild. That Saturday only one person, Dan from Los Angeles, spoke up.

"I want to hear how Tim's doing with his election."

Bless him. I wasn't going to bring it up, thinking they had already spent enough time in the meeting and everyone wanted to go home. But others spoke up then, too, and said they wanted to hear my report. I told them of my campaign fund's balance and my efforts to get a manager, of the coverage in the local paper and the buzz around the courthouse. Most of the Executive Board had already contributed and all voiced continued support, particularly the judge who'd been sitting to my right at the conference table all day.

"How did I not know about your election, Tim?" Ramona is one of the Los Angeles judges. "Who do I make the check out to?"

I started to give her the name and address to mail in a donation. Most people followed through.

"I'll just give it to you now and you can give it to your treasurer, if that's all right with you," she said as she pulled her checkbook out of her wallet. Apparently, Ramona's follow-through was not time-delayed. I saw a sizeable amount on the check she set down in front of me. "Let me know if you need more."

Every meeting Ramona and Dan and Ned and Kevin and people just like them reminded me how great it is to be able to work alongside wonderful people you can call not just colleagues but friends. In my own courthouse—and from courthouses up and down the state—people were watching out for me.

~

Chris the campaign manager had told me to wait before hiring him. Best to see, he'd said, if my opponent would follow through with the final paperwork to run a campaign or not. At one point it almost looked like he wouldn't. Judicial elections in California require at first an initial formal declaration of intention to run for office. Judges and challengers alike must file one. Even when there is no challenger, the judge still has to file the declaration if she or he wants to stay in office. To make sure no one acts frivolously, the declaration must be accompanied by a check in the amount of one percent of a judge's annual salary. My opponent filed that initial declaration and submitted the check early on. Then there's a two-week period for candidates to gather signatures from at least twenty registered voters who will nominate you to appear on the ballot.

I received encouraging news as the two-week period drew to its close. Walker had stopped by the election clerk's office the Friday before the nomination period expired and asked if it was too late to get his filing fee refunded. He was having severe second thoughts with the last day to submit his nominating signatures coming up that Monday. Someone had seen him in the elections office and called me at home that evening. The words "He's trying to cancel his campaign" washed away the usual clinging afternoon stress like a garden hose washing mud off my feet. When I'd picked up the phone, it had been a particularly rough feeling afternoon. The phone's ring made my skin crawl over muscle and bone at the thought of having to pick up and talk to anyone about anything. It was Friday afternoon and I wanted to hide, not talk. But I picked up the phone and I talked and by the end of the call the good news brought a message of respite and relief that calmed me more than anything had in days, in weeks.

It was more than merely feeling calmed down a few notches. It was as if I'd never felt any stress at all. None. No stress, no anxiety, no signs of depression. The switch had been flipped and that night was the first time I slept from bedtime until morning light since the reporter's first phone call.

The relief was short-lived. Monday after work I went to the election office in the county administration building next door to the state courthouse. Walker had filed his nomination paperwork and the campaign was on. I called Chris that evening with the news, trying to control the returning anxiety that put more thoughts in my head than my brain had room for. Chris said what I needed to hear.

"We'll meet for lunch and get to work. Time to win."

We met at a barbecue place a block from work. The prospect of meeting with Chris must not have daunted me because I showed up with an appetite. That's the thing about stress, anxiety and depression, at least my stress, anxiety and depression. They're not constant. It's one of the worst aspects of stress. It fools you into thinking things are getting better and then slams you into a pit you think is inescapable, lightless, airless, a choking darkness of unbearable weight.

But not that day. I ordered the half rack of ribs and finished them off along with the coleslaw and cornbread.

"I brought a contract for you to look at," Chris said, "along with a proposed schedule of milestones for the campaign."

The contract boiled down to his promise to handle the campaign as long as I would foot the bill for his services. The schedule covered when to order lawn signs, how many campaign mailers we'd try to appear on, the support he'd give for helping organize fundraising events—all of the things I didn't have the foggiest idea how to handle, he'd cover. I wasn't his only client that election season but he promised he could manage me quite well. I believed him, signed the contract, and told Vic the campaign treasurer to cut Chris a check for the first installment of his fee.

~

The odd thing about turning the campaign over to Chris is it's the exact opposite of how I run my courtroom. For court, I prepare for each hearing, read the briefs and motions, check the minutes from past hearings to see what has been accomplished so far, and walk into the courtroom expecting to be in firm control of the proceedings. It might be a day when I have only one case to address, like a jury trial, or a day when I have thirty or more cases to handle on pretrial motions and petitions and post-conviction sentencings and post-sentence probation violations.

No matter the case, they all need my singular attention. On the other hand, there are usually dozens of people in the courtroom waiting their turn. If these waiting people try to have a conversation while I'm hearing another person's case, I am invariably thrown off. I'm easily distracted from listening to the person addressing the court—a criminal lawyer arguing a sentencing issue, a small claims litigant trying to present their evidence, a prospective juror answering questions in jury selection—I'm easily distracted if someone else starts talking.

So, the rule is no one else talks.

In my courtroom, only one person speaks at a time and no one gets to interrupt anyone else. It's the same set of rules we all learned in kindergarten. They work well. But people who find themselves in court are usually nervous about it, especially if it's their first time. I explain the no-talking rule if necessary, and add that it makes the court reporter's job too difficult if someone speaks over another person. With jury selection I sometimes point out that the only person who gets to interrupt anyone else in the courtroom is me, but that's because I'm wearing the black robe and I have to keep order.

"I've tried wearing this around the house," I tell jurors, pointing to my robe, "but it just doesn't work with my kids."

The control I'm able to exercise in the courtroom—a tool for coping with and overcoming my distractibility—did not transfer to the campaign trail. Not in the slightest. There, I was not the one in control. I was not the one organizing the candidate forums. I was not able to put on my robe and force everyone into order. I had to trust Chris and others to guide me, and I had to find a way to concentrate despite the enhanced distraction that came with the stress of feeling out of control.

The first campaign event I'd planned to attend turned out to be the first I had to give up any hope of controlling. It was a large dinner affair held every election season that attracts local candidates and people at the state level, along with a few hundred supporters and potential supporters. My friend Tom had once chaired the committee that put on this political dinner and he'd promised to shepherd me through it, introduce me to influential people there, and talk me up among the voters. He ended up having to do a lot more than that.

The dinner fell on February 12th, Lincoln's Birthday. That was the morning I was in the doctor's office getting my pneumonia diagnosis. As my son Kyle drove me home from that appointment, I called Tom.

"Are you ready for the Lincoln Day dinner tonight?" Tom's voice always measured high on enthusiasm and encouragement.

"The doctor just told me I have pneumonia," I said. "I was hoping this was a cold and I'd be better by now but it's not. I'm not."

"Don't worry," Tom said.

"But dinner tonight . . . ."

"Don't worry. I'll go and represent you. It's early yet in the campaign. There's plenty of time later for you to contact people personally."

I didn't know if I believed him. This was still a bit before my initial phone call with Chris where he assured me of the same. But whether I believed him or not, I did trust Tom. He knew campaigning and I didn't. Plus, it wasn't like I had a choice. Physically—let alone mentally—I was in no shape to go anywhere. Once home, I made one more phone call before going to bed.

"Is Dave in?" I asked Leah, his wife. He wasn't.

"Should I have him call you?" she asked.

"It's about work tomorrow. I'm not going to be there." As that year's Presiding Judge of our local courthouse, Dave needed to know which judges were in and which were away. "The doctor just told me I have pneumonia." I was starting to get bored of saying that but to Leah this was news.

"That's terrible." Leah is not prone to understatement. "I'll tell Dave. You stay home and get better."

Later that day I saw an email from Dave. "I'm planning on you being out the rest of this week and probably the next. Don't worry about work. And don't worry about the election. If you're going to be laid out with pneumonia during a campaign it's better to do it in February than in April. There's plenty of time."

The verdict was in. Tom and Dave (who were on opposite ends of the political spectrum when it came to partisan politics but extremely experienced from years of campaigning) both said I'd be OK. I'd have to trust them even if I had no way of knowing for sure if it was true or not.

And that stressed me out.

∼

I got better pneumonia-wise and started attending events. That first was an interview with a local political committee, the same one that put on the big dinner I'd missed. A lot of candidates for a lot of offices on the local ballot were at the meeting hoping to get the committee's endorsement. I wasn't as much interested in obtaining their endorsement as preventing Jim Walker from getting it. The vice chair of this committee was one of his earliest supporters.

They let those running for most of the other offices go first. When it was time for the two judicial candidates, I'd seen that almost everyone was conversational about themselves and their bid for office. Humility and sticking to qualifications characterized the evening's discussions.

I did the same. I told them how long I'd been a judge, my experiences on the bench and in statewide judicial branch business, my non-judge community involvement, and that all my colleagues in the courthouse supported me. Then my opponent spoke.

"I helped Ronald Reagan win the Cold War."

Eyes around the committee table widened.

"As an Air Force navigator, I flew missions here in the U.S. and to Central America."

Flying missions from the States to Central America in the 80s. Was he claiming participation in the Iran/Contra Affair? We never found out. He soon switched gears and talked about his work as a prosecutor. They listened politely but the only person smiling was the vice-chair.

The chairperson called me the next day. "We decided not to issue an endorsement in the judicial race. Hope you understand."

I understood. My opponent had the vice-chair in his pocket while I had no one. It looked like the vice-chair could not convince the rest of the committee to join him, and I imagine for their part the others did not want to embarrass the vice-chair by backing me. The committee was neutralized and I counted that a win. What I hadn't counted was just how much of a win I'd achieved. A few weeks later I found out when I went into a local business owned by Nancy and Chuck.

"You impressed my son at that committee meeting," Chuck said.

"Committee?"

"The one all the candidates came to. He said you did well." I hadn't realized Chuck and Nancy's son was on that committee. "The guy running against you doesn't sound so hot. My son said it was the second time he heard him speak."

"Where else?"

"When he first announced his candidacy. My son was at that event too. He told me, 'Dad, every time that guy opens his mouth he sounds worse and worse.'"

I walked out of Chuck and Nancy's store feeling I'd definitely come out ahead at the committee endorsement meeting.

∽

More successes came along here and there. The Yolo County Bar Association held a forum where my opponent claimed "A killer is walking the streets because Judge Fall wouldn't let us use his confession." He was talking about a case he prosecuted in front of me a few years earlier. I was ready for his misdirecting rhetoric.

"I'm not the one who threw out the defendant's statement to the police," I explained when it was my turn to speak. "The court of appeal did that after Mr. Walker tried to use it in the first trial. They found the defendant's statement was obtained in violation of Miranda, and described circumstances I could see amounting to a coerced confession. They reversed the defendant's murder conviction from that first trial and sent the case back with the order to exclude the confession from the prosecution's evidence in the retrial. That's when the case first landed in my courtroom, because I didn't do the first trial." I looked around the roomful of attorneys. "And I know enough to follow the orders of a higher court in a retrial."

The attorneys nodded along. Most of them. Some instead glared at Walker.

"It's not as if the defendant got off free and clear in the second trial," I continued. "The prosecution put on the rest of the evidence and the jury convicted the defendant of manslaughter. Murder or manslaughter, it's a homicide conviction. I sentenced him to the maximum term. The man had been in custody from the date of his arrest, through the first trial, through the lengthy appeal, and through the second trial. By law, all of that time in custody is required to be applied to his sentence. Even with the maximum term imposed, he'd been in so long there were only a couple years left to serve until his release."

An experienced member of the bar association asked, "Did Mr. Walker petition the Court of Appeal to reverse your order to try to get the confession back in?"

Walker jumped in. "We considered it but decided to just go forward with the trial."

"So, you're complaining Judge Fall gave you a ruling you didn't like, a ruling you never took to the Court of Appeal, and then you got a conviction anyway?"

Walker sat down, silent.

The Yolo County Bar Association gave me its endorsement.

∼

One night, Liz drove from Davis to the county seat while I rode shotgun. This was one of the tips I picked up from the candidate guides: let someone else drive you to big events if possible. She pulled out of our driveway at 6:30 and we skirted the university campus as we took the freeway out of town, then north through the fields separating Woodland from Davis. The community center lies on the southern edge of town. She parked and helped me carry a few flyers and lawn signs inside where we saw the notice for the League of Women Voters candidate forum. The League held several of these forums every election year and that night they hosted me and Walker.

We entered the large hall. A camera from a local community access television station stood at the rear, the operator adjusting its height. Microphones on the tables in front were set so the candidates could be heard, and the room started to fill with more people than I had expected to show up to a debate on a judge's race. Liz was the only person there I knew. Then Walker arrived. Now I knew two people, one who wanted to take my job away from me.

I wandered to the back of the room and introduced myself to the camera operator.

"Are you here for all the debates?"

"Most."

"Hope I do all right."

He looked me up and down. "I've seen you speak before. You'll do fine."

Not so sure about that, I walked over to the moderator's table about the same time as my opponent. She explained the format: we would each make a statement, then the rest of the time would be spent answering audience questions. Every seat had index cards sitting on them and people would hand in questions to the moderator's table. She'd read them and provide both of us time to answer. Who went first alternated with each question. The moderator had a timekeeper who made sure neither of us rambled on too long.

Sounded fair to me. My opening focused on my experience while his was about how I needed replacing and he was just the guy to do it. The questions came in, and except for one on courtroom efficiencies and another on judicial demeanor I can't recall what any of the voters that night wanted to hear about.

"This next question is directed to Judge Fall personally. 'You have a reputation for being overbearing and short with people in your courtroom. How do you respond to that criticism?'"

"If by overbearing you mean I require everyone to act appropriately in my court, then I have to say it's true. And if being short means I don't let anyone, attorneys or others, behave in a manner less than what is called for in a courtroom, again I'd say that's right. I expect people to be on time, prepared, and to show courtesy to everyone else involved in a proceeding. No one gets to interrupt, no one shouts, and everyone will be given the opportunity to speak in their turn. What happens when someone can't follow these rules? I stop them. Running a courtroom takes concentration and diligence. That's what I bring to my job every day, and it's what makes it possible to give everyone a fair hearing on every case."

I sat down expecting the moderator to read the next question since, as she'd said, that one was directed to me personally. She picked up the next card to read when the timekeeper leaned over and whispered in her ear. The moderator looked at Walker. "Would you like an opportunity to respond to that question?"

"I certainly would," he said as he stood up. "What Judge Fall isn't telling you is how he berates lawyers, making them stand up in his courtroom and telling them to take their hands out of their pockets. It's like he has to prove to everyone that he's the one in control. I've seen him insist on getting his own way in court and shutting attorneys down. So many of them have told me about being victims of Judge Fall that I knew someone had to do something about it. That's why I'm running against him."

The moderator again picked up the next index card. I stood and asked, "May I respond briefly?" She looked relieved and nodded.

"I do make attorneys stand when addressing the court, and I do ask them to take their hands out of their pockets. Maybe it's because so much of my practice was in federal court, where formality is much stronger. But it works well. And as for getting my own way in court, when it comes to how the proceedings run isn't that what people expect from a judge, to be the one maintaining a sense of control? I must be doing it right, since the attorneys of the Yolo county Bar Association voted to endorse me and not my opponent. He hasn't even gained the endorsement of the prosecutors in his own office." I could have left that last part out, but it was too late. I'd said it, I stopped talking, and I sat back down.

It was Walker's answer to the question on judicial efficiencies that summarized the night for me. Someone had written "What are your plans to streamline court processes to move cases along faster?"

Walker went first and described a murder case that had not yet gone to trial after eleven years. "How is this justice for that man sitting in jail eleven years waiting for his day in court?" he cried. Walker promised he'd move it along once he got on the bench, claiming every judge in the courthouse was incapable of managing cases efficiently.

When my turn came, I explained to the group that I didn't know the details of the case he mentioned since it was not assigned to me. "But even if I were familiar with the case," I said, "I am barred by the code of judicial ethics from publicly commenting on matters pending in front of any judge, not just me. I can talk generally for you, though."

"Almost every time a case gets put over to another date it's because one or the other attorney needs more time, and it's as often the prosecutor as the defense attorney. I've granted Mr. Walker's motions to delay cases many times. It's fine if there's a good reason and, when there is, I give the lawyers the time they need. I don't necessarily give them all the time they're asking for, though. Just the time I think they need to finally be ready." That seemed like a good place to stop.

Walker stood up and said, "Let me tell you, folks. I'm not going to let something like judicial ethics keep me from telling you what I think!"

The room was silent. He rejected acting ethically? This was when I figured I probably won that night's debate.

~

The two of us met again when the largest newspaper in the county—the one the reporter Lauren writes for—invited us to meet with the publisher and the editor in chief. Again, we each made our pitch. Walker started by pointing out how another county newspaper once wrote an article critical of me. The editor in chief, Debbie, cut him off.

"We don't pay attention to what that newspaper writes."

He switched tactics and spoke of his own experiences in my courtroom, including the confession case, and what other attorneys thought of me.

"Have any of those other attorneys endorsed you?" asked Foy, the publisher.

"They're afraid to. Judge Fall is vindictive and they can't take the chance of angering him."

What my opponent hadn't counted on was that these newspaper people knew me. My wife and I had lived in Davis for decades, we raised Jenna and Kyle in Davis, gone to church in Davis, been part of the community. Vindictiveness was not what I was known for.

I alluded to my opponent's lack of local ties when talking about my own experiences when my turn came to speak. "I'm the only candidate who lives in this county. On top of my other qualifications, I've shown a commitment to this town and to the county."

Eventually the questions stopped and Debbie walked us out. I hung back a little as Walker stepped through the front doors of the news offices.

"Is his main point that you're strict with attorneys in the courtroom and you follow the law?" she asked. "Isn't that what people expect from a judge?"

"You'd think so."

"And he doesn't even live here?" She shook her head. "Foy and I will talk over the newspaper's endorsement and let you know."

Campaign

Debbie called me that night. I got the newspaper's endorsement.

That endorsement didn't surprise me, based on how the meeting went. What did surprise me was what came out of the other newspaper in the county, the one that had written such a critical article about me years before. Without calling me in for an interview, without so much as a hint they were even thinking of me, they threw their support behind me as well, calling me the most qualified candidate for the job.

Chapter 8

Self Care

EVEN WITH THESE CAMPAIGN successes I was not freed from anxiety. Starting with Lauren's first phone call and continuing incessantly until the night the polls closed (save for that one brief moment my opponent asked about getting his filing fee refunded), I battled the stress, the anxious voice in my head—that was my own voice—shouting at me, the depression that drove me to curl up on the couch on sunny Saturday afternoons. Every day, almost without fail, I had at least one episode. A lot of days it was endless and unceasing.

Medication helped. It's not a cure, but it helped. Once we got on the right anti-anxiety medicine at the right dosage—which took some time—the worst of the symptoms were tamped down. Most of the time. But tamped down doesn't mean gone, and there were times those symptoms roared.

Sleeping through the night was a constant struggle. I had medication for that too. It didn't work much. Waking up at 1:00 with my mind already racing with thoughts that had little to do with each other but everything to do with what I feared—or maybe thought I feared in the blackness of the night—those careening thoughts were more than a match for my sleep meds.

Some days were worse than bad. They were horrors. I didn't recognize how deeply they took me into my own private pit until one day in the campaign when I was distracting myself with the television and ran across the movie *Tommy Boy* as I channel-surfed. In the scene I landed on, Tommy (Chris Farley) and Richard (David Spade) are in the car. Tommy's life has not been going well. Then he runs over a deer.

He's done.

"Forget it, I quit, I can't do this anymore," Tommy says, each word winding him up tighter and tighter as his voice gets louder and louder. "My head's about to explode. My whole life sucks! I don't know what I'm doing, I don't know where I'm going. My dad just died, we just killed Bambi . . . and every time I drive down the road I just wanna jerk the wheel into a bridge abutment!"

I got Tommy. I got his words. I got how he felt. His voice sounded like mine sounds in my head. That was me. Did I want to drive into a bridge abutment? Did I?

That's when I realized I had considered it.

I wanted everything to end; I knew that. I wanted someone to make it all go away, but no one could do that. I wanted to quit if that would make it stop, but quitting wouldn't make it stop. Yet I did want it to stop, and I had wondered if there was a quick way to make that happen. Did I actually see a bridge abutment as the answer? No. Had I thought about whether a bridge abutment might be the answer? God help me, I had. Tommy Boy made me realize it, to admit it, to be honest with myself. I never told anyone else, not my doctor, not even my wife, until I wrote this book.

Troubles hide deep, and burdens buried within can crush from the inside out.

~

This was a problem. What was I going to do about it? I was already on my meds. They were helping. Much of the time. It depended on what time you were talking about. Some of my worst days came late in the campaign, but not as often as earlier in the campaign.

I was still in early days when I saw that scene in Tommy Boy. I needed to not indulge those thoughts. It wasn't a matter of banishing them from my head. Anxious thought is unbidden thought, thought that crashes through barriers I erected in my mind, thought that comes to settle in in the most unsettling way. Even though anxious thought came to visit, that didn't mean I needed to offer it my best chair and serve up something to feed upon.

One way I dealt with the stress, along with its fellow-travelers anxiety and depression, was to recognize them for what they were. Labeling anxiousness meant I could put it in its place. It might not go away, but anxiety and I both knew that it also wasn't here to stay. If nothing else, I eventually learned from experience that the passage of time would show it the door.

Exercise was another way to show anxiety the door. After the pneumonia recovery, I forced myself back to the gym in the mornings. I can't claim I made it every day, but I made it most days and soon nearly all. Lifting weights releases endorphins, I found, and those endorphins satisfied me. I also knew that feeling more satisfied, even to the slightest degree, is a better way to start the day.

We ended the day that way, too. It was Liz's idea. Every night, after dinner, we left the house with our dog Shasta—a rescue dog who as best we could tell was half Australian Shepherd and half Rottweiler—and took a walk around our quiet neighborhood. Usually it was no more than thirty minutes since we still needed to get home and go to bed early for the morning prayer/workout/ leave for work routine. Those walks, like walks usually are, were calming. We'd talk about the day. Hers, mine, the kids'—everything was up for discussion. As bad as afternoons were (and afternoons were always the hardest) those evening walks brought closure to the day.

What I put in my body was another change. I love coffee. Good coffee. Dark roast and strong-brewed coffee. Fully loaded with caffeine coffee. Caffeine was not my friend that campaign season.

Caffeine is a friend of anxiety.

If I drank coffee it immediately opened the door and invited anxiety to come on in and sit a spell. Caffeine will do that. It makes it extremely hard to tamp down the physical manifestations of anxiety when even a little too much caffeine manifests itself the same way. I gave up caffeine. No coffee. Plus, no Diet Pepsi. I love Diet Pepsi, too. No coffee and no Diet Pepsi for the duration. No sense putting out their welcome mat as an encouragement to anxiety. Anxiety didn't need any encouraging.

One self-medication people sometimes turn to when under stress is alcohol. It's one I was able to avoid as I haven't had a drink since I was 40 years old. Some of my friends are surprised to learn my decision not to drink alcohol isn't based on some sort of religious conviction. It's also not because of a health issue or an addiction. It's relational. When Jenna and Kyle were approaching their teen years, I knew they'd possibly—probably—wonder why I got to drink and they didn't. They each have a strong sense of justice and, like most kids, would think it arbitrary and unfair if Dad got to have a beer and they didn't. I wanted to take that conversation off the table, so I stopped drinking. Entirely. This meant no more craft beers (we have a lot of stellar microbreweries in Northern California), no more fine wines (we live on the edge of Napa's wine country), no more of the well-aged single malt Scotch I'd come to know and love from my student days at Sussex. I just stopped. When I finished the last beer in the fridge one day, that was it. By the time the election of 2008 came I hadn't had a drink in eight years and didn't think to start back up again.

I did drink a lot of water. Hot water. Just like old people, there I was at 48 turning on the kettle, heating up the water, and pouring it into my mug. I found it wonderfully relaxing, washing my insides like a warm shower washes outsides. Sometimes I'd add a teabag—herbal—but, as the weeks went on, I found myself opting for just the water, hot and in my mug. Drinking hot water like an old person. I liked it and it liked me. It's the Java Jive without the java.

∼

Television became part of my self-care too, especially in the early days when I stayed home sick and recovering from pneumonia. TV watching is part of who I am, as far back into my childhood as I can remember. The Monkees, Hogan's Heroes, Saturday morning cartoons. Now an adult and recovering from a major illness, I turned to TV. I needed something creative, not unnerving, and came to embrace the Disney Channel. Kim Possible, Lizzie Maguire, Wizards of Waverly Place, The Proud Family, Recess, and my favorite, Phineas and Ferb. Clever writing, good production values, and only enough cartoon angst to keep it interesting without revving up my own stress and anxiety.

Staying home sick and watching TV is a time-honored tradition in my life. When I was a kid, this included watching Dialing for Dollars, a local program combining old movies with a cash prize for a lucky viewer who was likewise home watching television when most kids were at school and many adults were already off to work. The host drew names and telephone numbers from a huge rotating bin and then thrust his arm into it up to his shoulder, rustling the paper scraps around before pulling one from the bottom. The names and numbers had been cut out of the telephone books from all nine counties in the San Francisco Bay Area. Viewers from Sonoma to San Jose might receive a call during one of the movie's commercial breaks. If no answer, the jackpot increased. If the person answered and could identify the amount of money in the jackpot, they won the prize. The most I remember anyone winning was $170, a staggering amount to a kid in the 60s. The host never called me.

The Dialing for Dollars opening theme song poked some good fun at the show's viewers as the Statler Brothers sang about counting flowers on wallpaper and playing solitaire all night long with a deck short one card, then catching Captain Kangaroo on the television as the morning wore on. It wasn't lost on me, even as a kid, that Dialing for Dollars immediately followed Captain Kangaroo on that channel. Nothing to do but watch daytime television? Like the song said: that doesn't bother me.

What did bother me during the campaign was asking people for money myself. It was the opposite of what the Dialing for Dollars television host did. Instead of calling people in order to give away money, I called people to ask them to send me money. After I'd been home with pneumonia for a few days I started spending part of the recovery time making a few phone calls to people I hoped would be supportive. I couldn't make many calls at first, as they wore me out both physically and emotionally, but I made a few from my sick couch in between Disney shows. I seemed to have better luck finding people on the phone than that television movie host ever did. Perhaps it's because people carry their phones with them now instead of leaving them tethered to their walls at home like when I was a kid.

"Hi, it's Tim Fall," I'd say. "I don't know if you heard but I'm running for reelection this year."

"I did hear," was a typical response. "How are you doing?"

During the early days I had a ready answer. "I'm home fighting pneumonia at the moment, but trying to make a few calls. I'm hoping you can help me out . . ."

I don't know whether it was sympathy for me being sick, a desire to help me keep my job, or a combination of both, but I got a lot of positive responses to those phone calls. That made for a nice boost to my self-care.

Chapter 9

The Fall Guy

I SAID MY NAME a lot during that campaign. Over and over and over. Events and meetings, the hundreds of telephone calls and face-to-face conversations, all of them required me to say my name. Emails too. A judge running for reelection has to put in the work to gather support. From endorsements to post on the campaign website to contributions for the treasury, from asking people to put up lawn signs or write letters to the editor of the local newspapers, I was constantly talking to someone. Talking, talking, and more talking.

"I'm Judge Tim Fall," I would tell people at an event. "I'm running for reelection."

"Hi, it's Tim fall," I'd say on the phone. "You might have heard I'm up for reelection this year."

"This is Tim Fall," I'd write in an email. "My reelection is coming around."

From there I'd ask for their vote, their endorsement, their money. Other than fund raising events where people already expected to be hit up for a check, I only asked for contributions from people I knew well enough to ask. Those were the most difficult conversations at first.

"Um, yeah, so I don't know if you'd like to contribute. I can give you the address of my campaign treasurer. No rush. OK, bye."

The more I did it the less awkward it felt. I figured if the people of this state have a law saying judges can be challenged for reelection then they must expect judges to be able to campaign to keep their jobs. Chris told me at our contract signing lunch that the campaign's cost would run between $65,000 and $100,000 depending on how much of a campaign my opponent mounted.

I started telling people that.

I closed every call with, "They say this campaign might cost up to a hundred thousand dollars. All I'm asking is for your best effort to help me cover that cost."

If they were interested, I told them how to send in a check. Most were interested. For face to face conversations I had pre-printed envelopes for them to mail in the contribution. No amount of money was ever mentioned beyond the projected campaign cost. How much a person gave, whether they were wealthy or living on a tight budget, was their call and I was not going to suggest that I expected any amount at all. Some gave small, some large, and some none. I raised enough to cover the cost.

For everyone who gave I again said my name, this time on a hand-written thank you note. One supporter later told me that instead of spending my time writing thank you notes I should have been campaigning and drumming up more support. For me, though, this was all part of a single campaign process; people were giving me themselves and I felt honor-bound to express how deeply grateful I felt. I still feel it.

Other people used my name as well, sometimes taking it in vain. It's one thing for my opponent to cast me, my actions, my words, my intellect, and my abilities in an unfavorable light. I expected as much and he didn't bother to hold back in those events we both attended. I could only imagine what he said when I wasn't there, and he certainly wasn't going to extol my virtues as he pursued his campaign strategies.

What I hadn't readied myself for were the baseless attacks from people who didn't know me, people who had never set foot in my courtroom. The worst was posted on a community forum blog. The writer accused me of bias in refusing to allow a same sex couple to adopt a child, ascribing my refusal to ultra-conservative religious beliefs. The only problem with the blog report is that it never happened. Never have I refused an adoption for a same sex couple. Rather, I've issued the decree of adoption for same sex couples on the same basis as anyone else. Sexuality is irrelevant.

Even more common than adoptions are name-change petitions, and they at times include issues where a person's sexuality is particularly relevant. In years where I handle the civil cases filed in our courthouse, several times a month I will hear people petitioning to change their names. Perhaps the person wants to remove the name of an abusive parent, or they want to honor their heritage, or they just like another name better. As long as the name change is not for an improper purpose, I grant the request.

I recall one young man who entered the courtroom for more than a name change. He also filed for change of gender, which is an official decree that a person's sex is no longer male but female, or vice versa. (Yes, gender and sex are not synonymous, but these are the words the statute uses.) Some more conservative Christians might ask how a judge who is also a Christian is supposed to handle a request from someone seeking to change their legal identity from male to female or female to male. I've been asked the same about signing divorce decrees and performing same sex marriages. We address these cases as we would handle anything else in the courtroom. By being fair and respectful to everyone who comes before us.

I called that name and gender change case by using the petitioner's original name, Mr. _____. He came forward, smiling but (like almost everyone who's never been in court) a little unsure of what to do. I pointed out where he should stand at counsel table and asked him to wait a moment while I looked through the file. I'd reviewed it earlier, but I always double check name change petitions to make sure the person filled out the paperwork fully and correctly. He listed his current name and the name he wanted to change to, and he checked the box showing the request to change from male to female for all legal recognition. Attached to the petition was the required doctor's statement affirming that changing the sexual designation was medically appropriate.

Everything was there so I granted the petition, including an order that the government issue a new birth certificate reflecting the new name and sex. And since this was an official act, my next statement to the petitioner was, "Ms. _____, you need to take the order I've just signed to the clerk's office downstairs. They'll give you a copy with the court stamp on it for you to keep."

"Thanks." She gathered her paperwork and left the courtroom with the same smile I saw when she had first approached the counsel table.

~

What I called myself during the campaign was more important than I realized. Did I want the formality of my full name and title? "I am Judge Timothy L. Fall, and I humbly seek your heartfelt support for my reelection as a Superior Court Judge." That is a mouthful. Did I want to appear approachable and accessible by going casual? "Hi, everyone! I'm Tim and I'd like to keep being a judge!" All I knew was that I didn't want to get *too* familiar with people; after all, no one but my Aunt Mickey called me Timmy after I turned thirteen. Getting the name right was important, not only for talking to people one-on-one but for my lawn signs and for the formal statement I needed to draft for the official ballot pamphlet the county elections office mailed out to everyone registered to vote that year.

Too long (Judge Timothy L. Fall) and I'd come across as stodgy and stuffy, which even in a judge is undesirable. Too short (Judge Fall) and it would sound like an incomplete sentence. Getting my name right was key. I've been trying to get it right all my life.

You'd think having a last name like Fall would make life easy: it's short, easy to read and pronounce, not at all confusing. You might think that, but you'd be wrong. We have to spell our family name all the time. Here's how Liz usually does it: "My last name? Fall . . . like the season. F-A-L-L." I tend to take a different tack: "Fall . . . as in fall in, fall out, fall off, fall over. Fall. [sigh] No,

Fall. F-A-L-L." That's how it usually goes over the phone. Talking to people in person doesn't necessarily make it any easier. Once I went to a store to pick up a watch we'd left for repair.

"I think you have something ready for me? The last name is Fall."

The clerk checked the bins behind the counter. "I don't see anything here. What was the name again?"

I enunciated with what I considered astonishing clarity. "Fall."

"Sorry, nothing here," said the clerk, checking the same bins again. "Did we call you to say it was ready?"

"Yes." I surprised myself by being nowhere near as exasperated as you might expect. "We left it here a few days ago and you called yesterday. It should be under Fall."

"Sorry sir." The clerk checked the same bins again, I think just to humor me. He turned back to look at me. "We don't have anything under the name of Fong."

Decades earlier an even more disparate name swap occurred. I was walking to school when I was a kid, maybe 10 or 11 years old. I always wore this oversized jacket and stuffed my hands way down in the pockets. This day was no different.

Across the street and behind me a little bit I heard some girls talking loudly. One of them said, "Is that Murray? Hey, Murray!"

I wasn't Murray. That was the last name of another guy at school. I knew who the girls were, though, having caught a glimpse of them a half a block earlier. A couple of them were in my grade and a couple of them were in the grade above me with Murray. They were the cool kids. You could tell because they called people by their last names. Not only was I not in their crowd, but I was certainly not the type of 10-year-old guy who talked to girls easily. I did what any other kid like me would have done in that situation. I shoved my hands deeper in my pockets and hoped they'd forget they ever saw me.

They didn't.

"Murray! Hey, Murray!"

This went on for almost a full block.

"Murray! Hey, Murray!"

I kept wanting them to stop.

"Murray! Hey, Murray!"

They didn't stop.

I came to an intersection and stepped off the curb, my ears ringing with "Murray! Hey, Murray!" When I'd neared the other side, one of the girls said to her friends, "That's not Murray. That's Tim Fall."

They finally got it. Maybe that would make them stop. Nope. Raising my foot up onto the curb, this is what I heard.

"Hey, Fall!"

My toe caught the curb, pitching me forward with my hands deeply jammed into the oversize coat's pockets, as I did just as they'd commanded from the other side of the street.

I fell.

I'll leave to your imagination my frame of mind for the rest of that walk to school.

~

"Tim Fall or Timothy L. Fall?" I asked Dave, my politically savvy colleague, about the official ballot statement.

"Tim Fall. Keep it simple. Nobody identifies with a Timothy."

"Got it. What about listing my occupation under my name? Superior Court Judge or Judge of the Superior Court?"

"Nobody cares." Dave was not only politically savvy but direct. "As long as it has Judge in it, you're fine."

I went with "Tim Fall" and can't remember how I listed my occupation. Dave was right. No one cared, including me.

Chapter 10

Home Stretch

"Can you ride in the Youth Day Parade again this year?" asked Mike.

Mike was the City Treasurer for the City of Winters, a community of a few thousand in the far west of the county. He chaired the Youth Day Parade held every April. For Winters Youth Day, high school students take on roles as counterparts to local leaders: youth mayor, youth police chief, youth fire chief, and more. The one position that isn't found among the local officials of the City of Winters is a state court judge, so they reach out to the courthouse a few miles northeast. Winters has had a Youth Day since the Depression, a day designed to encourage, support, and celebrate kids of all ages. The big event capping off this celebration is the parade where the youth officials share cars with their adult counterparts as they ride down main street and wave to the crowds on the curbs.

In 2008 Winters had about 7000 residents. The number lining the parade was closer to 10,000. The youth officials' cars are joined by floats and dance troupes, Shriners on go-karts and caballeros on horseback, with marching bands from the elementary school, middle school, high school and UC Davis interspersed to provide a moving soundtrack. For the people of Winters, you are either in the parade or watching it. And if you're in the crowd watching, you're there alongside friends and family who came in from out of town to watch it with you.

My first Youth Day Parade was in 1996. I think the generically worded letter inviting someone to take part must have landed on my desk as the most junior judge in the courthouse at the time, and I was expected to make an appearance for the court. I went, I rode, I loved it. I told Mike the next week to send me the invitation every year because it was a blast. When 2008 rolled around and he called asking if I could ride in the parade again, I gave my usual answer. Then I asked, "Is there a chance you could mention my reelection when we pass the Grand Marshall's stage?" Mike always stood on stage in the most thickly crowded part of the parade route and announced each entry as it passed by.

"Sure, no problem. I'll come up with something."

A few weeks earlier I'd included almost all the Winters officials in my campaign phone calls. Some I knew and some not, but the phone call was the same. "Hi, this is Tim Fall from the courthouse in Woodland. I'm up for reelection and am hoping for your endorsement. I've enjoyed the Youth Day Parade rides with the youth judges the past twelve years." By the time I got that far they were ready to say yes. Winters people love their Youth Day. Mike was the first person I called early on, and turned out to be the most effective Winters supporter once Youth Day arrived.

The parade starts at 10:00 on the fourth Saturday of every April. I parked my car in the staging area around 9:30 and found my friends Steve and Carmina who always volunteer with organizing the entries. They walked me to the right spot and introduced me to the youth judge and our driver. At 10:00 the cars and floats far ahead of us started crawling forward and eventually we pulled out to join the string of parade entries. We rode the route sitting up on the back seat of the convertible and waved to the crowd, just like every year.

The first year's parade occurred about nine months after I took the bench. I was still getting used to the role of judge and this was my first big public event since taking office. I brought my robe and a spare I'd borrowed from a colleague so the youth judge could look judicial, too. We wore them as we traveled along the parade route.

For years, my wife was more likely to be recognized around town than I was. If someone stopped me in a store I could expect to be asked "Aren't you Liz Fall's husband?" But in 1996, wearing my robe, riding in the parade sitting in a car with my name posted on the side, cruising slowly down Main Street in a town a few miles west of where we lived, I thought I'd certainly be seen as Judge Fall.

That's how it went for a couple blocks. People called out "Hi, Judge!" or yelled encouragement to the Youth Judge. Truth be told, a lot more people called out to her than to me. Then again, she was a local. Still, a few said "Hi, Judge!" as we passed. Yes, I was there in my own right. We were nearing the Grand Marshall's stage and the crowd grew thicker. I heard the entries ahead of us being announced and thought, "They're going to say my name, too. That'll be nice."

Then I heard it. Not from in front where Mike stood announcing the entries passing in front of him, but from behind me. The noise from the crowd ebbed and flowed as we crawled along and, in a moment when it died down more than a little, a woman we'd just passed yelled out for all to hear, "Hey! Aren't you Liz Fall's husband?"

I looked over my shoulder, waved, and yelled back the only response I could. "Yes! Yes, I am!" The stage announcement for my inaugural appearance in the Winters parade moments later ("Let's welcome Judge Tim Fall and our youth judge _____ _____!") was anticlimactic.

By 2008 the people of Winters were used to me. A lot of waves, a lot of smiles, and a lot of friendly shouts accompanied the youth judge and me as we rolled down Main Street in our robes. We reached the Grand Marshall's stage where Mike announced my high school counterpart and me.

"Let's welcome our youth judge and Judge Tim Fall," Mike said, just like every year. I figured that was it. I was wrong. There was more: "We'd like to thank Judge Fall for his many years of support for Winters Youth Day and for participating in the parade once again this year. We wish him great success in his reelection, too. Thank you, Judge Fall, for all you've done for Winters!"

As campaign endorsements go, that was a good one.

~

April is the month to push the lawn signs. After the parade, another Winters official said he'd take twenty and hand them out at a barbecue he and a bunch of civic leaders were going to in the afternoon. My friends Carmina and Steve—along with a few other Winterites—said they'd take even more and get them up around town. Winters and the entire southwest corner of the county would be well covered.

On the east end of the county I had another offer to get multiple signs up. My brother had married into a West Sacramento family and his wife's parents and siblings have lived there for years. When her brother found out I was up for reelection, he said, "You have campaign signs in the car? Give me twenty. I'll get people at church to set them up." He must have found a ready crowd because a week later he asked for ten more. More West Sac people joined in to get my signs up and soon every neighborhood in town was fielding signs calling for my reelection.

From one end of the county to the other—north, south, east and west—I wanted my signs up and visible to the most traffic. I told my friends, "Intersections are best, through roads and streets are good, too, but even down a cul-de-sac is better than not having a sign there at all." We have miles of rural roads connecting the communities of our county. Getting signs posted, especially on the main roads and crossroads, was key. Of the six hundred signs purchased, I handed out four hundred fifty. Most of them found a spot somewhere, whether high-trafficked or a trickle.

In May, the first of the campaign mailers went out and I kept making phone calls. The mailers were effective enough that some of the people I reached by phone mentioned them.

"Nice picture of you and Liz and the kids. Haven't I seen it before?"

"That's from our vacation in Bodega Bay a few years ago. We used it for a Christmas card." Using older photographs saved the campaign the expense of paying for professional studio time. My own picture was up to date, and that's what featured in most of the campaign literature. It was good to show people my graying hair. They expect that in a judge. It hadn't always been gray, as a friend reminded me once.

~

Cindy and Rick are a little bit older than Liz and I, with kids who were in high school when I was sworn in as a judge. Cindy and I served on the church committee that recruited our senior pastor back in 1992, but by the late 1990s she and her family had moved to Missouri. Cindy occasionally returned for visits, and on one she kindly reminded me of my advancing age and unavoidable mortality.

"Welcome back to Davis," I said as she hugged me in the church courtyard. She pulled back, tilted her head to the side, and reached her hand up by my ear.

"Whaddya know," she said as she brushed the hair at my temple. "Gray hair. You're finally starting to look like a judge."

I'm so relieved that happened before I had to ask people to vote for me.

~

The month of May also meant more fundraising. On top of the personal phone calls ("I'm asking for your best effort"), some lawyers who supported me—and definitely did not want to see my opponent on the bench—held events in their offices.

I pulled into a downtown Sacramento parking garage as most cars were pulling out for the evening. Stepping from my car, I hauled some campaign signs and flyers out of the trunk, found the elevated walkway to the high-rise office building next door, and took the elevator to the office where Steve, Roger and Bob put on an after-work reception for attorneys to come by and hear what I had to say. I gave my stump speech, but since most people there already knew me my efforts weren't as forceful as when I was in a roomful of strangers. I finished my remarks, thanked them all for coming, and stepped back with a smile thinking it was time to resume mingling, especially since two of my old law partners came to support me. Out of the corner of my eye I saw Roger stepped forward.

"You've heard why we should support him," he said, "but what Tim is too nice a guy to tell you is why we need to make sure his opponent is not just defeated but by an overwhelming margin." He was detailed, forceful, and brief, all the qualities that make him one of the best attorneys I've ever seen in action. There was no mudslinging; just facts and a conclusion. Most days the afternoons and evenings were the hardest part of the day. Not that one. I drove home to a late diner, appetite intact and mind set at ease by Roger, Steve, Bob, and all the people who came to support me at the reception.

Ten days before the election another firm held an event, this time in Jim and Dave's converted Victorian that held their offices a block off Main Street in downtown Woodland. I stood on the front porch greeting everyone as they came up the steps. Tom, a local politician, rode his bicycle down the street. His office was around the corner and he looked to be headed toward his house a few blocks away. I didn't expect him to attend my fundraiser. He liked me well enough, but when I'd asked for his endorsement back in February he turned me down flat.

"Sorry. Walker worked on one of my campaigns." That was it. Politics prevented considering supporting me even though Tom admitted I was better qualified. "I'll have to stay out of it," he said. "I can't give an endorsement either way."

Neutralizing an endorsement for your opponent was better than nothing so I thanked him and hung up. Now, three months later, there was Tom bicycling home from his Main Street office. We made eye contact as he came down the road and I waved while he smiled up at me.

My host Jim called out over my shoulder, "Hey, Tom, wait up!" Jim hopped down the steps while Tom put on his brakes and stopped at the curb.

I couldn't hear their conversation, and didn't want to put Tom on the spot by going down the front walk to join them. I focused my attention instead on the arriving supporters who were pausing to say hello and wish me well before entering the old Victorian in search of drinks and hors d'oeuvres. Jim later found me inside.

"Great turn-out," he said with a huge smile.

"Thanks for hosting this. You're very generous to invite everyone here tonight."

"Speaking of generous, Tom told me to give you this." I looked down at his hand. He held a folded-up check. "He has to attend another event tonight."

I didn't look at the amount. I didn't have to. A check from Tom meant he'd moved from neutral to support. That meant more to me than any amount of money.

Chapter 11

Election Day

My colleague Kathy cut short a trip out of town to host my election night gathering in her home. She recommended a caterer, Liz and I met with him, and the final plans for the night the balloting closed were in place.

Those final days were brutal. Most days had been a fight to lock up the incessant yelling in my brain, but now the days became a fog: clouded thinking, constantly forcing myself to concentrate rather than give in to distraction, to focus on even the simplest of tasks, finding myself wondering what I had been doing one moment prior—that was how I spent the week leading up to Election Day. The only comfort as I saw that day approach was that it would all be over soon. This was the one coherent thought I could latch on to. Still, it wasn't as bad as those earliest days. I slept through the night now once in a while and I could eat normally most days. Afternoons were still the worst when it came to controlling stress and there were still days where the only way to manage my anxiety was to hole up by myself in a quiet room.

Quiet was my constant craving. Emotional quiet. Physical quiet. Noise quiet. I'd spent countless hours being shouted at by my brain, my body, my emotions. It was a completely permeating noise. I'd only felt a noise that permeating once before in my life.

~

Years ago, before kids, Liz and I went to Germany to visit her sister and brother in law. Kim and Bob lived in a small village on a hill a few miles from Ramstein Air Force Base. To get to the village you left Ramstein, drove through a small town, then a smaller town, then a village, then a smaller village, and eventually you wound through the hills to Kim and Bob's house on top of a ridge with a tiny collection of other houses for neighbors. Their village was so small that while it had a bakery you needed to visit the next village over to get milk from the dairy. The dairy village people in turn had to trek to Kim and Bob's village to get their bread. Their house proved a small, quiet, and very rural retreat from the bustle we were used to in California.

Bob flew F-15s for the Air Force. Toward the end of our visit his squadron flew out for an extended mission, and Kim asked if we wanted to watch the take off. The main airfield wasn't available for the squadron's departure that day, so we parked near an auxiliary air strip and climbed up the small control tower and entered the compact control room. Unlike the main air field, this control tower was placed right on the single runway which stretched down a cleared strip of ground, a line of trees on either side. One of the squadron's pilots, acting as liaison officer to the control room operation, met us inside. The tower operators were all non-commissioned officers.

"Sergeant, can you put the radio traffic on the speaker for our guests?"

"Yes, Captain." The sergeant barely looked up. She and her team focused on the dials and gauges and instruments before them and on the airstrip just the other side of the tower's glass walls.

We soon heard a pilot announce he was awaiting permission. The sergeant directed the pilot to enter the runway and, when he was in position, gave permission for take-off. The jet slowly appeared far to our left and came toward us. The accelerating speed of approach was startling and by the time it reached the tower midway down the runway the jet's wheels were off the ground. The engine's roar shook the tower. Plane after plane took off—"There goes Bob!" Kim said over the noise—until eventually just one remained.

"Anyone want to go out on the catwalk for the final take-off?" asked the liaison pilot from Bob's squadron.

"You should do it," Kim told me.

The sergeant opened a door at the end of the instrument counter stretching in a half circle from left to right across the glass fronting the tower's control room, at the point where the glass met the metal walls that formed the rear of the tower. A narrow catwalk ran the half circle around the front of the tower's glass walls.

"Stand over here, a little to the side," the squadron liaison said as he ducked back inside and closed the door.

The last jet appeared far to my left and picked up speed. The roar of the engine grew and I realized how insulated from sound we'd been inside the tower. Closer and louder the jet grew until it reached the tower and rose off the ground a couple dozen feet from where I stood on that exposed metal railing. I no longer heard the noise. Instead, I felt it, my sense of hearing overwhelmed by the soundwaves, my body rocked to its core by the passing jet. I'd been hit by a wall of sound shaking me where I stood.

Grinning, I went inside. "That was incredible."

Enjoying the experience of overwhelming soundwaves isn't for everybody. The same goes for the experience of judging. Judges hear cases every day that would overwhelm most people. People come to court because something awful has happened in their lives or the lives of people they care about. Families break down, businesses fall apart, auto accidents maim or kill, children suffer horrific abuse at the hands of those they should be able to look to for comfort and loving care. I hear these cases constantly, sometimes in explicit detail as the witnesses testify. People ask how I can stand it. All I can say is that I am built this way. I can listen to disputes, give everyone a fair chance to be heard, and deliver judgment based on law. I've done this for years and never found myself overwhelmed by stress on the job.

A lot of people would feel like I did on that catwalk after just one day in court, only instead of grinning at the experience they'd find themselves wracked physically, mentally, emotionally. The stress of the campaign hit me like that wall of sound and I crumpled under it, a pile of broken me, laying in a heap, wanting only to crawl away.

That's the way it felt almost every day in the beginning. By the end of May, those days were fewer. Still, I couldn't face thinking what would happen to my mental health if I lost the election. So, I chose not to think about it. One way I coped was to take some vacation days. From the Friday before the election to the Wednesday afterward I was off work, giving my courtroom responsibilities a rest.

More phone calls came in to me than I made to others in those final days. People wished me well and asked if there was anything left to do. "Just tell your friends to vote for me," I'd say with as much cheer as I could muster. There was no sense putting up more lawn signs, and it was too late to send in more letters to the editor. The newspaper had plenty in their queue and kept publishing them right up to the day before the election. Those letters encouraged me greatly. Whether they persuaded anyone is beyond my knowing, but if the volume of letters encouraging voters to cast their ballots for me reflected the community's support generally then I was doing OK. The ratio of letters on the subject of the judicial race ran nine to one in my favor.

Lawn signs ran similarly. Walker had a few dozen up in Woodland, the county seat, but I had more there. In Davis, the largest city in the county, as well as in Winters and West Sacramento, you'd be hard pressed to find one of my opponent's signs in anyone's yard. The same held for the miles of country road stretching between the cities and the smaller towns and crossroads throughout the county. Mine didn't go up all at once but over a two and a half month effort they went up all over. That was a boost not only for the campaign but for my own moods.

Encouragement is a good stress ameliorator.

～

June 3, 2008, arrived. A Tuesday. Election Day. Liz and I had already voted, just like every year, turning in our ballots directly to the elections office in the county administration building next door to the courthouse a few days early. I voted for me. I'm fairly confident Liz did too.

On Tuesday afternoon we went to the caterer to pick up the food for the election night gathering at my colleague Kathy's house. Of the trays and trays of food we loaded into the back of our ten-year-old minivan, the only items I recall with absolute certainty were the oversized Rice Krispie squares packed with huge shards of dark chocolate. There were plenty of upscale food choices on the other trays, but I had insisted on this dessert. I know my comfort food and if there was ever a night I needed some, this was going to be it.

"It's open!" Kathy yelled as we knocked on her front door. Her house was only a few blocks from ours. "Back here."

We followed her voice and found her in the kitchen.

"Is it too early to set out the food?" We'd arrived about 6:00 and the gathering was set to begin at 7:30, shortly before the polls close.

"Everything can go on the table and sideboard in the dining room." She pointed and we turned to see a beautifully appointed table with a centerpiece of dried flowers, along with matching décor on the sideboard.

With a few trips back and forth we emptied the minivan and covered the surfaces in the dining room. Kathy approved the layout of finger foods, savory and sweet.

"That should please people," she said. "Come check the drinks." The kitchen counters were covered in water bottles and wine bottles. Cases of soda rested on the floor next to large, brightly colored plastic tubs with rope handles.

"Where do you want the ice?" came a yell from the front door.

"In the kitchen!" answered Kathy.

A woman and man each carried twenty-pound bags of crushed ice into the house. "There're three more bags in the car. Do you think that's enough?"

"Should be," Kathy said. She introduced us to her friends before they went to retrieve the rest of the ice. "I recruited them as co-organizers," she told us. "You and Liz need to concentrate on guests from here on out."

We poured ice in the tubs and added soda cans and water bottles. "OK," I said. "We're going home to change. Be back soon."

The simple chores of unloading the van, setting out the food, and working shoulder to shoulder with Liz had completely distracted me from the fact this was Election Day, but there was no avoiding the fact it was fast becoming Election Night. Even with the polls closing we had to be on our game for the rest of the evening.

~

As we pulled up to Kathy's house in separate cars (I imagined staying into late hours if necessary and Liz had to go to work the next day), we saw she'd transformed her front yard into a forest of campaign signs, each one urging people to "Re-elect Judge Tim Fall" in bold red letters next to a silver gavel on a dark blue background. There would be no doubt which house on the block was hosting my election night party. The thing about going to election night parties, though, was you didn't know if you were there to celebrate or commiserate. For me and Liz, we were waiting to see if anyone would show up either way. It was close on 7:15 when we arrived and, other than Kathy and her helpers, we were the only ones there.

"Plenty of food for us," I said in an effort to joke away the stress that had been building since we'd gone home to change. People lose elections, my brain kept telling me. Judges lose elections. *You* could lose, my brain specified. My body reacted in kind.

There was nothing I could do about the election by now. The polls closed at 8:00 and my efforts were either enough or they weren't. That's what Liz kept telling me. Plus, her usual reminder.

"This is in God's hands. It always has been. If you stay with this job, you do. If you move on to something else, he's with you there, too."

I told myself that all the time. I still wasn't sleeping through the night some nights, my appetite wasn't back to full bore, and my body felt like it wanted to burst out of my skin most days, even at that late stage of the campaign season, but Liz was with me to hold me up. God was using her to be strong for me.

As I stood looking at the tables full of food and the house empty of people, the front door with its "Please Come In" sign tacked to it opened wide. "You can't miss the party house!" Leah announced as she walked in.

"I didn't know you had that many signs left," Dave said. "There must be hundreds up all over the county."

"I stockpiled a few for party decorations," Kathy said.

Dave and Leah's arrival opened the floodgates. By 7:45 at least 50 people had arrived, many I knew personally or from the campaign's email list used to send out invitations to the party, but there were also people I didn't know. I didn't even recognize their names handwritten on the tags they'd fill out on the welcome table in the entryway. Dave cleared up the mystery.

"People involved in local campaigns like to go where the winners are on election night, even if they don't know you," he said. "That's why they came here."

"I haven't won anything yet."

"You will," Leah said, "and they know it."

I hoped they were right. A few people who'd come to wish me well made a brief appearance and left for other campaign parties, making the rounds. Some who had started elsewhere popped in to Kathy's house after a while. I shook a lot of hands and received a few hugs. I'm not a hugger of people I don't know well, and I'm not effusive with my body or my words, but I managed to say "Thanks for coming" and "Thanks for your support" or sometimes just "Thanks."

Only one guest left me standing speechless and motionless.

∿

A few years before the campaign I'd handled the family law assignment for the courthouse. Marriages breaking down, families in crisis, parents splitting up, adults no longer able to work together in the best interests of their children (let alone each other's interests), property disputes, wage garnishments, or house sales.

It's a heavy assignment. Recesses in the courtroom proceedings are often necessary to take a quick respite from the turmoil inherent in child custody disputes and marriage dissolutions. One day I stepped off the bench and into chambers, picked up the phone on my desk, and dialed.

"Hey," I said.

"What's going on?" Liz asked. "You don't usually call this time of day."

"I just need to talk to someone whose marriage isn't going down the tubes."

"You called the right person." Liz once again proved she's strong enough to support me if I feel worn and weary. God's blessing. Plus, I was glad to hear she too thought ours was a marriage not going down the tubes.

One of the guests at Kathy's house on election night was Marion, a woman whose divorce I had handled during that family law assignment years before. Her case wouldn't have been memorable except for one hearing in particular during her marriage's breakup. Her husband, Stan, asked for an early decree of dissolution so the marriage would be legally terminated while the court retained jurisdiction over all the money issues: property division, spousal support, distribution of retirement benefits, who gets the house. It's not unusual to enter the dissolution decree ahead of the judgment on the rest of the issues, but occasionally it's best to wait and do it all together.

I found that theirs was one of those occasional cases and denied early dissolution. Marion was relieved at the order. It wasn't that she had hopes of saving the marriage; she knew it was over. She just thought that if the divorce part came in early then he would not be as motivated to get the money matters resolved as swiftly. There was another woman, though, who was not pleased with my order denying early dissolution: Beth, Stan's fiancée. I later found out that Beth and Stan had their wedding already planned and set a date based on the expectation I'd grant the early divorce. When I didn't, all plans were off. Beth did not like that one bit, as I later found out firsthand.

I crossed paths with all of them in one way or another during the campaign season those many years after the divorce proceedings. Marion made first contact. She was on Dave's email list and responded immediately with an endorsement and an offer to take a stack of lawn signs to place in friends' yards around town.

Stan and I next ran into each other when I attended a Veterans of Foreign Wars pancake breakfast. One of my supporters was a long-time member and suggested I come along so he could introduce me to potential voters. Stan was working in the kitchen. As I made my way down the line, he and I made eye contact. I recognized him. Stan is pretty well-known as a civic leader in our community. Deciding I had nothing to lose, I asked for his support. He immediately gave it to me, along with a big smile. Maybe ruling against him years earlier wasn't a sore spot with him.

Beth was the last I came in contact with that spring and it was in the courtroom, not the campaign trail. I was in the middle of jury selection when the clerk called a few more people into the jury box for questioning. Beth gave her full name.

"Are you Stan's wife?" I asked.

"Yes."

"Counsel," I said, turning to the attorneys, "please give me a moment to put a brief disclosure on the record. I don't want to get into too many details, but I handled a case years ago that involved this juror's family." Then I returned my focus to Beth in the jury box. "You're aware your husband is supporting me in my campaign for reelection?"

"Oh, I'm aware," she said, glaring. "We had a long talk about it." I got the impression Beth had not yet let bygones be bygones when it came to having her wedding plans ruined.

Of the three—Marion, Stan, and Beth—Marion was the one who made it to Kathy's house on election night. (Not that I expected Stan and Beth to attend, although they belong to the same community service club Kathy is in.) Marion caught me as I walked through the crowd from the kitchen to the living room. I repeated the phrase I'd said a dozen times.

"Thanks for coming tonight, and for all your help on the . . ."

Marion grabbed my shoulders, leaned in, and kissed me on the lips. Not a handshake I could return nor a hug I could tolerate, but a kiss. On the lips. She planted it smack on my smacker and made sure it stayed there.

I broke off as best I could without shoving her to the ground. I looked around. No one was staring.

"Glad to help," she said. "You're a good judge." Off she went through the crowd.

And off I went to find Liz. She advised I not get face to face with Marion again. So to speak.

～

At 8:00 a handful of people went into the den off Kathy's living room and turned on the computer to check the county elections office's website. Once polls closed, the vote tallies started getting posted. At 8:01, we found, no precincts had reported.

"Don't worry," one of the veteran vote watchers said. "They usually don't post anything before 8:15. The first returns will be the mail-in ballots they've already processed."

I went back to my guests. "Nothing yet," I said.

Liz was talking to Kim and Scott, our friends from church. "They're going to wait a few more minutes for the vote count," Liz said, "but they have to get up for work tomorrow."

So does everyone else, I thought as I looked around the room. The people who spent every election campaigning for themselves or someone else's bid for local office weren't in a hurry to go anywhere, though. Now that poll results were imminent they hunkered down to get the news from the election website as soon as it posted.

A couple people kept watch at the computer and hit refresh every minute or two. 8:15, 8:20, 8:25—no results yet. Then, a minute or so before half past the hour, a yell came from the den.

"They're in!"

Tunnel vision cut off everything around me. I tried controlling my breath and not sound like a boy hitting puberty, my voice jumping registers mid-word. "How does it look for me?"

"You're ahead," they said.

"Can I see?" I took a look but the computer screen was already on one of the other races they were following. A hand reached over and clicked on the button to bring up my race. The initial results showed I had 74% of the ballots.

"That's mostly the early voting," Dave said over my shoulder. "Your numbers probably won't stay that high. But you won. He can't catch you."

Liz pulled me to one side. "Congratulations. I knew you could do it."

I'd had my doubts, I reminded her. "Thanks for seeing me through this," I said in her ear to cut through the noise in the room as more results were being shouted from the den to the rest of the house. The place was more crowded than it had been just fifteen minutes earlier and everyone was catching the new arrivals up on the incoming results for the races.

My phone rang. It was Lauren, the reporter.

"Congratulations. Do you have a quote for tomorrow's paper?"

I hadn't thought about the press. "Can we go off the record for a sec while I ramble and try to come up with something judicious to say?"

"Absolutely. Let me know when you're ready."

We made small talk about the campaign for a couple minutes. "OK, I'm ready."

"Shoot."

I said something about looking forward to continuing to serve, about my gratitude to the voters and everyone who supported me, about the responsibility I felt to do my best on the bench. When I read it in the paper the next day, it looked quite judicious.

My phone kept ringing. People who couldn't make the party called to congratulate me, telling me they knew I had it in the bag all along. None of them knew the overwhelming doubts I'd battled, the stress and anxiety. My body was still feeling the effects, still feeling like my skin didn't fit, like my chest was too tight and my legs too loose. But my brain was quiet. Between the noise from the party, the phone calls coming in, and the election results shouted from the den, I didn't have brain room for racing thoughts.

"There's an update!" someone yelled from the den.

My numbers had changed, rising from 74% to 75.2%. That was unexpected.

"I'm going to see if Kathy wants me to stay and help clean up," Liz said. She had to get up for work too, and wanted to hit the gym beforehand. We checked with Kathy.

"This mess? I'm not touching it tonight." She pointed at her friend. "This is our project for tomorrow evening over a bottle of red."

We offered to return to help. Kathy was having none of it. Kathy's no means no, I've learned over the years we've worked together. I walked Liz to the door and out to the minivan.

"I think I'm here until the crowd goes home. Don't wait up. I'll probably try to sleep in in the morning."

"I figured." We kissed and I watched her drive off.

By 9:30 the house was empty. Despite Kathy's protests, I stacked leftover sodas and water bottles on dish towels on her kitchen table and emptied the ice from the large plastic tubs outside. The June night was warm enough that it would all melt and evaporate by morning. My brain and body's stress felt like it was finally starting to do the same. I went back inside.

"The food's gone," I said. "What do you want me to do with the aluminum trays?"

"Nothing. I have a box full of trash bags and we'll get to divvying up the recycling from the trash tomorrow."

"Thanks." I stood leaning against the back of a chair. "All of this. It was great. You're great."

"It's what we do for each other. Now, we got this. Go home to Liz."

Chapter 12

Aftermath and Lessons Learned

AVOIDANCE IS A COPING mechanism. It's not a good one, but it's a method. I mastered quite the ability to avoid over the course of the campaign season: people, phone calls, emails—I could avoid almost everything. That's not bad over the short term where it gives a person space to rest, regroup, or reconsider realities. Long term it stagnates, stultifies, and stalls out any hope of improvement. My campaign season consisted of alternately compelling myself onto forced marches and retreating as far from the conflict as possible. Of all the ways I tried to cope, avoidance was my specialty.

The morning after Election Day I was avoiding waking up. Which was odd. I'd spent the past four-plus months unable to sleep through the night, jumping from deep sleep to utter wakefulness in a moment and then staring at the ceiling until dawn, my mind racing with worry over all the things I could do nothing about in the middle of the night.

That morning I awoke well after sunrise, and I realized as I did that my eyes hadn't opened all night, not since the moment my head hit the pillow late the evening before. I left my head right there on that pillow while considering this: I slept through the night. And my body felt odd. Something was different.

What was that feeling?

Rested. I felt rested. It's a state of being I hadn't felt in months. It was unfamiliar, but I thought I could find a way to get used to it again.

Liz was gone for work already. I hadn't heard her get up for the gym and I hadn't heard her come back to get ready for work, having slept right through. I rolled out of bed, skipped shaving, and threw on shorts and a T-shirt. I'd already put in for a vacation day, after all. If I'd lost the election, I knew I'd be in no shape to handle being in the courtroom. Since I won, I was grateful for a recovery day before getting back to work.

Sitting down to the computer, I opened the elections page to see if my lead had held up. With all the precincts tallied, the results came in at 76.5% for me, meaning my opponent received less than a quarter of the vote. In addition to listing each precinct with its vote breakdown, the elections office posted precinct maps of the three largest cities with color coded ballot results. Precincts that voted for me were green and those that voted for Walker would be red. Would be. In the City of Davis where I lived, every precinct showed green. For West Sacramento, all green. And in Woodland where my opponent had his most visible support? Every precinct went to green. Not a single precinct in any of the three cities went his way.

Seeing the numbers broken down throughout the county's rural precincts, seeing the maps glaring bright green in the cities, all this brought home to me that the victory was real. If the website had included a map of Winters and the smaller towns and communities it would have been even greener. Every city and town in the county broke my way. It brought a whole new meaning to the phrase "go green."

After breakfast—a hearty and thoroughly enjoyed breakfast—I drove out of town onto the county roads. My signs stood at crossroads and down narrow lanes, in front of wheat fields and walnut orchards. At each sign's posting I pulled over and tossed the sign into the back of my car. People in the cities could walk out their front doors and pull the signs out of their yards. I wanted to save the farmers and ranchers who allowed my signs on their property the trouble of tracking them down.

Our county roads are on a one-mile grid system. East/west roads start with County Road 1 at the northern county line, while north/south roads start with number 41 on the western edge of the county. In theory this would mean that every square mile of the county would be neatly bounded by roadway: County Road 28 is one mile north of County Road 29, with County Road 96 on the west of the square being one mile from County Road 97 to the east. Being an agricultural region with irregular county borders, the occasion for a single mile to separate one intersection from another does not work out as consistently in practice as it does in theory. Plus, if there's an extra road in between to reach homes that are not a full mile apart, you end up with a County Road 97, then 97A, and eventually 98. It makes for giving interesting directions to people visiting from out of the area.

I drove County Road 105 and 84, 32 and 24. Skirting Winters (73.5% of the vote) and on through the tiny crossroads of Madison (77%), one campaign sign became ten, and ten became fifty. A few miles up the Capay Valley, as I approached the western border of the county, I stopped seeing signs. I didn't make it as far north as Knights Landing (80%) or as far south as Clarksburg (77%); it's a big county and I was hungry. Turning back down the Capay Valley I stopped at the Burger Barn in Esparto (72%) for a late lunch. I pulled into a shady place to park and walked to the window that hung over the edge of the small asphalt parking lot.

"A cheeseburger and fries please. And a chocolate shake." Burger Barn had the best shakes in the county. A table stood nearby under a spreading oak tree. I likewise spread the cheeseburger's wrapper on the table and spilled some fries onto the waxy paper. The cheese was gooey, the burger well-charred, the fries properly greasy, and the shake just about thick enough to stand on its own outside the cup if necessary. It wasn't necessary. I wolfed down half the shake, shoved a fistful of fries into my mouth and chewed swiftly so as to clear enough room for a largish bite of the burger to cram into my gaping maw.

~

I've always liked small-town hamburger joints. Yakima in central Washington was a sleepy town in the 60s, and much different from the stretch of northern California coastline where I grew up. Cold in the winter and hot in the summer, that's what I remember about Yakima from when I was a kid.

We had family there, so every couple of years we loaded up the wagon and rented a trailer to haul behind us and drove a couple of days to get there. My grandparents lived in a little house well-situated for a kid like me, because less than a stone's throw from their front porch was an A&W Root Beer stand. This wasn't like one of those fast food restaurants you see nowadays. This was a place where you walked up to the counter under an awning, ordered your hamburger and root beer and sat down to eat at a picnic table outside. Or at your grandmother's house if she was practically next door.

I drank a lot of root beer when I was at Grandma's house.

I was 6 when my grandfather died, and my grandmother moved in with my aunt and her family. That was in a different part of town, so going for visits didn't include as much root beer drinking. Grandma remarried a few years later, deciding to spend her days with an old family friend who was also widowed, and moved out of her daughter's house. Her new home was back on the same street as the root beer stand, but a lot more than a stone's throw away. Ten blocks were much too far for a kid like me to walk on my own.

I was about 12 when our summer visit coincided with my Dad's cousin, Jack, being in town visiting family too. Cousin Jack was a bit older than Dad, and he'd never lost the cowboy drawl that characterized the older members of our family, which traced itself to a 19th Century homestead outside Sheridan, Wyoming. Jack always looked and sounded like he just rode off the range from a cattle drive.

I must have looked and sounded like I was bored silly sitting there outside my grandmother's back door, because Cousin Jack sought me out.

"Tim, d'yew lack root bahr?"

Root bahr. I knew what he meant. "Yes."

"Hawp in thuh truck."

I hopped. Cousin Jack's pickup truck had seen the other side of a split rail fence, that's for sure. He started it up, let the clutch out as he eased it into first gear, and drove down the road. The further he drove away from Grandma's house, the closer we got to that oasis of froth.

And soon we pulled up at A&W.

Cousin Jack asked the woman at the counter for a gallon of root bahr, and she turned to pull the handle on the tap to fill a glass jug with the heavenly nectar.

Back in the truck we went, and drove to Grandma's. Once there, Jack said, "Hep yuhsef, Tim."

"Do you want a glass, Cousin Jack?" I said, remembering my manners.

"No thanks, Tim. I cain't drink thet stuff."

Two things about that: first, my 12-year-old self couldn't believe there was anyone on the planet who didn't drink root beer; second, I suddenly realized that Cousin Jack had bought a gallon of root beer just for me.

I was almost speechless, but managed to come up with "Thanks, Cousin Jack."

Back then I didn't have the word for what Cousin Jack did for me, but I do now. His act was extravagant. Jack bought something he didn't need and couldn't use, and he did it for me. And he bought more root beer than I'd ever had, all to myself.

His actions remind me of Jesus.

I have a Savior who paid for something he didn't need. He paid for the forgiveness of sins he didn't commit. In his extravagant grace, he offered his own body, his own blood, his very life, to set me free. Jesus paid that price for me and then he said these wonderful words, words I didn't even know I wanted to hear.

"Tim, you are mine. Forever mine."

Forever his. And now I drink from a fountain that flows from within me, one that leaves me never thirsty again but always wanting to drink more of my Savior.

Thanks, Jesus, for the example of Cousin Jack's extravagance to a 12-year-old boy, and for seeing me through that election season as well.

～

Waking up after an uninterrupted election night's sleep; passing through the beauty of wheat fields and strawberry fields, orchards and vineyards, cattle ranches and sheep pens; and savoring a burger at a roadside stand in a town of three thousand people a stone's throw from the banks of Cache Creek. I'd forgotten days like this existed, that they were possible in my life. Maybe other people had them, but not me. Yet here it was and I was in it.

Slurping the last of the shake, I crumpled the burger and fries wrappers into a ball, took the lid off the cup, crammed the wrappers inside and tossed it all into the trash can. I put the little red plastic wicker basket on the counter by the take-out window and walked to my car. The French have a phrase for my mood: bien-être, well-being. That was me. My mind, my body, my emotions, my soul was bien-être all over.

As I drove the county's backroads home, I felt a yawn coming on. It wasn't stress. I was just tired.

～

The courthouse parking lot stood empty as I pulled in early the next morning. I walked across the street into the historic neo-classical building, swiped my keycard on the side door, climbed the granite staircase up two stories, crossed the marble walled foyer of the third floor and slipped my key into the lock of the frosted glass door into my chambers. My clerk's desk had a couple of file folders open on it. My desk, as I saw in turning the corner into my office, was buried in files.

I had a full calendar ahead of me that day.

Usually I would have reviewed the files the day before and come to work fully prepared for the thirty to fifty cases set for hearing in my felony courtroom each morning. Sentencings, probation reviews, pretrial motions to suppress evidence or disclose it, these and more are common. Theft, drug dealing, armed robbery, domestic violence, homicide, auto burglary, and gang crimes were typical for a busy felony judge to consider from day to day. Only when I'm in trial do I have the luxury of concentrating on one case at a time, but then it is total concentration on all that is going on with that one case.

Unlike the logistics of a reelection campaign, organizing my caseload comes easy to me. I'd done it for years by then and I was good at it. I sat at my desk, pulled out a pad of sticky notes, and started with the case on top of the first pile of folders to my left. Working down that stack and then moving to the next and then the third pile, I soon had a note stuck to the front of every case.

"NSP, 3 yrs UBT susp, Res Tx" my first note read—No state prison (NSP) at the outset of sentencing meant this was a sentence on a plea agreement where the defendant would receive a probation grant with a three year state prison sentence suspended pending successful performance while on probation (UBT representing the upper base term for that particular crime) plus a referral to a residential treatment program (Res Tx) for a drug addiction. If the person made it through probation successfully, the three-year prison term went away. If they didn't, the probation grant could be terminated and the person would serve their time in prison.

"PX, 211 2nd, 1538.5"—A second degree robbery charge (Penal Code section 211) was set for a preliminary examination (PX) that day to determine if there was enough evidence to order the defendant to stand trial. Penal Code section 1538.5 indicated a motion to suppress evidence, which is typically heard concurrently with the preliminary examination; if the evidence is ordered suppressed it is less likely the court will find there is enough evidence left to order a person to stand trial.

"TRC, 6/9/08 JT, 5 days, DV"—a trial readiness conference (TRC) for a five-day domestic violence (DV) jury trial (JT) set to begin that following Monday, assuming both sides confirmed their readiness for trial at this final status conference. My courtroom schedule is set to hear trials one week and do all my pretrial and post-trial hearings the next, and so on back and forth. Most trial weeks have several cases set because not every case will be ready on the date originally chosen. If more than one case turns out to be ready to go to trial, we try to find an open courtroom for it. Most felony trials take only three to five days but if it's longer we readjust workloads to free up a judge and courtroom to go into the following week for the rest of the trial.

These were the types of hearings I prepped for between 7:30 and 9:00 my first morning back after the election. I then stepped onto the bench.

"Remain seated and come to order," the bailiff said. I had asked my bailiff to stop using "All rise" years before, the morning I saw a man in a wheelchair left sitting while everyone around him stood for me to take my place at the bench. Now the call to order always includes the instruction to remain seated.

That's what the bailiff said as I entered the courtroom my first day back after the election. "Remain Seated and come to order. Superior Court Department Two is now in session, the Honorable Timothy L. Fall, judge presiding."

That was me. I was still a judge, and would remain so for at least another six-year term. The crowded courtroom came to order as instructed and we got down to business. A small group of defendants sat in the jury box to my left wearing jail jumpsuits with shackles on their feet and a belly chain linking them to one another. The bailiff had written their names out for me so I could call the cases of those in custody first. Once completed with that group of people, I turned to cases with people sitting in the audience area of the courtroom who were appearing out of custody. The initial group of in-custody defendants would be returned to the courthouse's main holding area and the next group would be walked up to my courtroom to occupy the jury box. I'd then address their cases, return to those out of custody, and back and forth until there were no more cases left to call. That could take a while.

A half-dozen prosecutors and even more defense attorneys did their best to stay organized as we called one case after another, skipping down the list, then back to an earlier case, and somehow made our way through the morning calendar. With every case I finished I handed a file to my clerk and moved to the next. One by one, all the file folders moved from my bench to my clerk's desk. Once my bench was empty, the morning was done.

My opponent Jim Walker entered the courtroom midway through this first morning back. He approached the team of prosecutors from his office and leaned down to say something. He must be passing along a message, I thought. Perhaps there's a case needing someone's attention in another courtroom. I knew Walker couldn't be making an appearance in my department since I had recused myself from all his cases as soon as he announced his candidacy against me. It doesn't look good for a sitting judge to preside over cases where one of the lawyers is trying to take that judge's job away.

He chuckled as he spoke to one attorney, smiled at another, then stepped around counsel table toward my clerk's desk and asked me, "May I approach?"

That was odd on two counts. First, attorneys in my courtroom know I don't like sidebar discussions and I grant them only rarely and only if absolutely necessary. Criminal hearings are open to the public and I consider that the public has a right to see and hear all the proceedings, every aspect. Second, and even more important, Walker didn't have any cases in my courtroom. There was nothing to approach the bench for on that busy Thursday morning.

"I'm in the middle of my calendar," I told him and pointed to the stack of files still sitting on my bench. I called the next case and kept moving.

The next day I ran into one of the supervising prosecutors who had supported me in my race. We paused to say hello on the courthouse steps as the lunch hour began.

"I heard you had a visitor in court yesterday," he said.

"Jim Walker? Yeah. That was weird."

"He was bragging to everyone the day after the election how he was going to walk into your courtroom, come straight to the bench, and shake your hand for all to see, like it would show everyone what a good sport he is."

"It was a stunt? If he wants to talk to me, he can catch me in my office on a recess. Why did he think it was a good idea to interrupt a busy calendar?"

"Who knows, Judge? It's just one more indication he doesn't understand what it takes to sit on the bench."

I didn't see my opponent in my courtroom again but a few days later we ran into each other in the third-floor hallway. No one was around.

"You're a hard man to get hold of," he said.

"I'm either on the bench or in chambers."

"Anyway, congratulations."

"Thanks." He turned away. "Wait a sec," I said. "The final report on campaign finances is due. I submitted mine yesterday." Missing filing deadlines means incurring a fine. "I don't know if you have the deadline marked down yet." I knew he'd already had to ask for an extension for one of the interim finance reports midway through the campaign.

"I didn't, Thanks."

We haven't had more than a handful of encounters in the years since. He left the District Attorney's office and started practicing criminal defense in Sacramento about a year after the election. From what I hear, it's going well.

~

Robert Redford's character in his 1972 film *The Candidate*, Bill McKay, is recruited to run for United States Senator against an incumbent who is considered unbeatable, and McKay's party wants to mount a campaign merely to make a showing. The hopeless campaign turns into a real political race, though, and then the race turns into a surprising victory. Stunned on election night, McKay drags his campaign manager aside and, with a look of complete bewilderment on his face, delivers the film's final line: "What do we do now?"

It's a good question for anyone who's won an election. The world says "Get your act together" and all I can think some days is "I'm supposed to have an act?" But it's not really about having your act together. Like the rest of life, it's all about people.

"Maybe you'll understand people in your courtroom better," Liz reminded me.

I had just finished describing for the twentieth time the relief I felt. My doctor weaned me off the anxiety medicine, my appetite returned, weight was coming back on, and sleeping through the night was a regularity. From the night we saw the election returns come in, all my symptoms turned off like a switch. No stress, no anxiety, no depression, no lethargy, no screaming in my head.

All gone.

"Lots of people in court have mental illness," I said. "But I can't give them breaks just because they've got depression."

"You can understand them," she said. "You might be the only one in the courtroom who can."

She was right. Judges are allowed, and sometimes required by the code of ethics, to accommodate the needs of people in court. Anxiety and depression come with needs. We can accommodate those needs by taking breaks, giving someone extra time to consider a plea bargain, allowing them an opportunity to gather their thoughts to express themselves more clearly—all of these wreak havoc on moving a busy calendar along quickly, but they can all be required for a person to have a fair hearing.

That's what Due Process is about: notice and an opportunity to be heard. Notice means making sure a person knows what's going on in a hearing, and the opportunity to be heard means giving people a fair opportunity to have their say. Going through my battles has helped me do the job of providing Due Process better, and not just when someone with a mental illness is in the courtroom. Language barriers, transportation problems, overworked attorneys, and understaffed court divisions are a few of the opportunities for me to slow down, be patient, and give people space to get their job done or say their piece. A rush to judgment is no way to be fair, and rushing staff or attorneys or witnesses is no way to be a judge. I have to balance all that with the need to keep matters moving so everyone appearing in court that day will get their case heard. As one of our retired judges was fond of saying about hearing a morning full of small claims trials, "Everyone is entitled to their day in court. They're just not entitled to a full day in court."

I still expect a lot from the attorneys who appear in my courtroom. As I often tell law students, the secret to having a good day in court is to be on time and be prepared. Even if you lose the case at least you'll know it wasn't because you failed to put in the work. I try to model the same by preparing for hearings and starting on time. On the rare occasions I don't start on time, I apologize to those I've kept waiting in the courtroom and explain the delay: reviewing a last-minute request for an emergency protective order, perhaps, or taking a phone call over the recess from a judge in another part of the state who needs urgent ethics advice on a case they're about to handle in their own courtroom. I've found that people kept waiting appreciate it when they know what's going on, even if it made me late to start their own cases.

That's part of the ethic that drives us as judges, both informally out of our notion of fairness and formally in the set of state regulations known as the California Code of Judicial Ethics: "A judge shall dispose of all judicial matters fairly, promptly, and efficiently. A judge shall manage the courtroom in a manner that provides all litigants the opportunity to have their matters fairly adjudicated in accordance with the law" (Canon 3B[8]).

Yet Canon 3's call for efficiency and promptness does not excuse impatience or unfair practices: "The obligation of a judge to dispose of matters promptly and efficiently must not take precedence over the judge's obligation to dispose of matters fairly and with patience. . . . Prompt disposition of the court's business requires a judge to devote adequate time to judicial duties, to be punctual in attending court and expeditious in determining matters under submission, and to require that court officials [i.e., employees], litigants, and their lawyers cooperate with the judge to those ends" (Canon 3B[8], Advisory Committee Comment).

Patience is a fundamental requirement not merely for the judge but for all involved: "A judge shall be patient, dignified, and courteous to all litigants, jurors, witnesses, lawyers, and others with whom the judge deals in an official capacity, and shall require similar conduct of lawyers and of all court staff and court personnel under the judge's direction and control" (Canon 3B[4]).

Failure to abide by these and other canons of ethics can lead to investigation and disciplinary action from the state's Commission on Judicial Performance, perhaps even removal from the bench. My own struggles—like the rest of my life's experiences, from parenting to leading worship music in church to teaching judicial ethics to rooms filled with judges—have given me a better understanding and a broader awareness of how I can fulfill my ethical obligations on the job. That's not always easy.

~

You'd think courtrooms can be formal and stuffy places, right? Serious business goes on there and everyone is on their best behavior at all times, aren't they? Would anyone act inappropriately? You'd be surprised.

In almost two and a half decades of judging, I can say that many of the people who enter my courtroom are models of professionalism and good citizenship. These are the ones who make my job easier, a pleasure in fact. There are exceptions, though, and these are the times my dedication to the canons of ethics is put to the test.

IT'S IMPOLITE TO BE IMPOLITE

Years ago, a man making his first appearance on a criminal case stood next to the bailiff, handcuffed and wearing a jail jumpsuit. I asked if he could afford an attorney. He said no. I offered to appoint one for him.

"Sure, whatever falls off the dump truck."

"Sir," I said, "we don't disparage anyone in the courtroom."

He immediately looked down, embarrassed.

"Sorry, I didn't mean any disrespect."

It's probably one of the most repeated lessons we teach children: "If you can't say something nice, don't say anything at all." Or as Peter put it when quoting from Psalm 34, "Whoever would love life and see good days must keep their tongue from evil and their lips from deceitful speech" (1 Pet 3:10).

WAITING YOUR TURN

I've handled small claims cases along the way as well. No lawyers are allowed, and the people involved have scant familiarity with courtrooms. What little they think they know is what they've seen on the daytime judge shows on television. I try to explain the process in real courtrooms as clearly as I can, but things still get a little out of hand at times. One side will be presenting their evidence and the other won't be able to keep from blurting out "But that's not true!" They then commence talking over one another just like they've seen people do on daytime television.

I stop the proceedings. I point out that I can only hear from one side at a time, but they will get their chance and, when they do, I will make sure the other side does not interrupt them. It's like when my kids were younger and they'd play pin the tail on the donkey or have a piñata at their birthday party: "One at a time . . . everyone will get their turn . . . don't shove your way to the front of the others." One thing we judges are supposed to do well is make sure everyone gets their turn. Scripture says it's good to wait until everyone has a chance to speak: "In a lawsuit the first to speak seems right, until someone comes forward and cross-examines" (Prov 18:17).

INSIDE VOICES, PLEASE

Even attorneys can lose their cool. If one side thinks the other is taking an unfair position on a case, it can irk them and occasionally they let it show: their voices get louder, speech comes more rapidly, and (dare I say it?) someone sounds a bit whiny.

I will occasionally hold up my hand like a traffic cop, lean into the microphone, and say quietly, "Counsel, petulance is rarely a persuasive form of argument."

Sometimes they stop and look at me quizzically, trying to sort out the twenty-dollar words in that sentence. This is usually enough of a break to get them off their irked-ness and back on a more productive track. Again, it reminds me of lessons we teach our children who can get frustrated much more easily and whose voices express that frustration in louder and louder tones so that parents need to calm them. "I can hear you better if you slow down and use your inside voice." Paul says this about keeping a cool head: "Do not think of yourselves more highly than you ought, but rather think of yourselves with sober judgment, in accordance with the faith God has distributed to each of you" (Rom 12:3).

TIME FOR RECESS

Judges can get out of hand as well. Whether it's someone in the courtroom who is punching every button I've got and getting on my last nerve, or a trial that has exceeded its time estimate for the third time, or just fighting an ultra-nasty head cold that has me completely out of sorts, I know I can skate to the edge of uncivil behavior myself (and I've even slid right over the edge, too). When I see it happening, I put myself on time-out. Happily, I can do that. It's called taking a recess, and rest is good. Jesus said so in Matthew 11. "Come to me, all you who are weary and burdened, and I will give you rest."

◦◦

I've found that carrying out the ethics canons or applying my life-learned parenting skills in the courtroom is consistent with the fruit of the Spirit of God: love, joy, peace, patience, kindness, goodness, faithfulness, gentleness, and self-control (Gal 5:22–23). As Paul wrote, "Against such things there is no law" (Gal 5:23). It's precisely when I most exhibit the fruit of the Spirit that I am best able to follow the law found in the Code of Judicial Ethics and to use the experiences God has brought me through.

How might that reveal itself on any given day? Finding joy in my job; fostering peace in a contentious hearing; speaking kind words to an overworked member of courthouse staff. Even in the midst of the most horrific cases imaginable, this is my job.

I'm glad I have it. The job seems to suit me. And going through that election—even with the stress and anxiety and depression, the sleeplessness and pneumonia and weight loss, the near-daily mental and physical and emotional battering—has made me better at it.

Epilogue

A Parable and
an Encouragement

THE PARABLE

There once was a person who had anxiety. Bad anxiety, the kind that keeps you from living like people who don't have anxiety.

The anxiety wasn't because of a lack of faith. The person praised God daily and trusted God even when it seemed God was far away.

The anxiety wasn't a sign of a bad prayer life. The person prayed for God's help, and gave thanks for God's provision.

The anxiety wasn't punishment for sin. The person knew Jesus bore the punishment for every sin, and that God never condemns his children.

The anxiety hurt and it made life hard, but the person refused to let other people make life even harder by insisting all the person needed to make the anxiety go away was more faith, more prayer, and to stop sinning.

The person found a good doctor and relied on good friends. That helped make life not so hard.

∾

THE ENCOURAGEMENT

Anxiety and depression do make life hard but there are ways to address them. If you think you've recognized yourself in some of what I went through, you're not alone. One in four people deal with anxiety, depression, or both at some point in their lives, either chronically and persistently or occasionally and episodically as I did.

One in four people.

That means that even if you never face anxiety or depression in your own life, someone you know will be, has been, or now is dealing with it. Count on it, you know someone with Generalized Anxiety Disorder or Persistent Depressive Disorder or one of the related conditions. You might not yet know that about your friend, your family member, your co-worker, but it's a fact of life for people around you right now.

One benefit of having dealt with this in the election of 2008 is that when I next felt anxiety overtaking me again eight years later—caused by the stress of my father at the age of 92 going into emergency neurosurgery, then the need to take on the duties of moving him out of his apartment in the Bay Area and into an assisted senior living community in our town, managing his finances, medical care and well-being for the next three years—when I felt overwhelmed by that stress and anxiety I knew to get on it right away.

I went to the doctor a few days after Dad's surgery, explained my symptoms, and immediately started on medication. I also took leave from work to reduce the stressors. Driving two to three hours to and from the hospital and then the rehab facility four to five times a week for the entire month of August 2016 was wearing enough; sleeplessness and appetite issues returned as well to compound my brain's and body's stressors. But because I got help early this time, the intensity wasn't nearly as severe. I knew I'd get through this, too, based on my earlier experiences. It was a matter of time and circumstance.

That's what happened. For me anyway. No one's anxiety or depression will look like mine or anyone else's. What is common is that treatment and friends and self-care help. Don't listen to those who tell you it's all in your head, as if thinking positive thoughts will stop the disease. They don't know what they're talking about. If you're a person of faith, don't listen to those who insist your health issues are due to a lack of faith. Those people don't know what they're talking about either.

Listen to your body. It's telling you you're sick. Do what you would with any other illness. Get help, rest, let other people come alongside you, and see a doctor. It's OK. It's OK to talk about it and it's OK to do something about it.

And it can get better.

Postscript

THERE HAVE BEEN TWO more election cycles since that campaign, 2014 and 2020. No one filed to run against me either year. I'm still a judge.

CPSIA information can be obtained
at www.ICGtesting.com
Printed in the USA
FSHW021257011221
86614FS

9 781725 260870